The Keys to Effective Schools

nea
NATIONAL EDUCATION ASSOCIATION

EDITED BY **WILLIS D. HAWLEY**
WITH DONALD L. ROLLIE

The Keys to
Effective
Schools

EDUCATIONAL REFORM AS
CONTINUOUS IMPROVEMENT

nea
NATIONAL EDUCATION ASSOCIATION

CORWIN PRESS, INC.
A Sage Publications Company
Thousand Oaks, California

For information:

Corwin Press, Inc.
A Sage Publications Company
2455 Teller Road
Thousand Oaks, California 91320
E-mail: order@corwinpress.com

Sage Publications Ltd.
6 Bonhill Street
London EC2A 4PU
United Kingdom

Sage Publications India Pvt. Ltd.
M-32 Market
Greater Kailash I
New Delhi 110 048 India

Printed in the United States of America

Library of Congress Cataloging-in-Publication Data

The keys to effective schools: Educational reform as continuous improvement / edited by Willis D. Hawley, with Donald L. Rollie.
    p. cm.
    Includes bibliographical references and index.
    ISBN 0-7619-7939-9 (c.)—ISBN 0-7619-7840-2 (pbk.)
    1. School improvement programs—United States. 2. Teacher effectiveness—United States. 3. Learning.   I. Hawley, Willis D.
II. Rollie, Donald L.
    LB2822.82 .K493 2001
    371.2′00973—dc21   2001002188

This book is printed on acid-free paper.

        03   04   05   06   07   7   6   5   4   3   2

Acquiring Editor: Rachel Livsey
Corwin Editorial Assistant: Phyllis Cappello
Production Editor: Olivia Weber
Editorial Assistant: Cindy Bear
Typesetter/Designer: Rebecca Evans
Indexer: Juniee Oneida
Cover Designer: Tracy E. Miller

Contents

Preface
The Problem of School Improvement

Donald L. Rollie
Quality Schools, Research and Policy
National Education Association

S ince the turn of the last century, there have been a series of cyclical reform efforts beginning with acute criticism and exposé reports, followed
by an intensive search for workable solutions. In most schools, innovations
tend to appear and disappear with a disturbing regularity, sometimes simply under different labels. Few reforms persist long enough to greatly affect
the educational system. Reform approaches have been simplistic and
inconsistent. Reformers have not strategically used what we have recently
learned about how the best schools achieve superior results.

Increasingly, educational researchers and policy analysts agree that the
organizational design and culture of schools can either enhance or hinder
their effectiveness. They argue for a shift to more supportive leadership,
more participative decision making focused on student achievement and
collaborative action. Organizational design features can increase worker
motivation and result in increased productivity, especially in organizations
that depend on worker commitment and expertise for successful task
accomplishment.

This book offers a series of chapters by some of our best education
thinkers. It is designed to provide ways that parents, educators, and policymakers might understand and solve those organizational problems that get
in the way of student achievement. These concise research-based chapters
are written around the framework of the KEYS initiative of the National
Education Association (NEA). KEYS, a shorthand for Keys to Excellence in
Your Schools, is a program that is based on a careful and thorough inves-
tigation into how the organizational and culture features of a school can

affect student achievement and how changing a school's structure and organizational patterns will improve the quality of teaching and learning experienced by all the school's students.

Although this book was originally commissioned to support the adoption and implementation of the KEYS initiative, the lessons the chapters in this book teach apply to any effort to improve schools in fundamental ways. The research cited in this introduction and in the chapters demonstrated that securing and sustaining the essential characteristics of effective schools that make up the KEYS should be at the heart of school reform and will result in schools capable of continuous improvement.

Over the past two decades, America has become preoccupied with quality. Quality has been the subject of discussion in business and industry, in the military, and in the service sector. Inevitably, quality has become a topic of discussions in education, as it should. The questions being asked include, can schools, and especially public schools, become learning organizations? Can we teach others to create and sustain high quality schools? Can we create an instrument, like a thermometer, to allow a school to check its own organizational health?

The KEYS Initiative

From the research that undergirds KEYS, we learned that quality schools consist of many characteristics, and we identified principles that can be used measure quality. Ways of identifying how schools measure up provide schools with tools they can use to improve teaching and learning conditions. Schools that consistently displayed multiple characteristics of quality, which we call indicators of school excellence, promote high student achievement. But we also learned that to achieve total quality, all of the characteristics must be present, and in large quantities. These characteristics, or indicators, cluster into six broad factors, which we call KEYS. Each KEY factor will be addressed in whole or in part by one or more of the chapters that follow. The six KEYS are as follows:

- Authentic, Learner-Centered Instruction
- Shared Understanding and Commitment to High Goals
- Open Communication and Collaborative Problem Solving
- Continuous Assessment for Teaching and Learning

- Personal and Professional Learning
- Resources to Support Teaching and Learning

The KEYS initiative provides participating schools with a survey and follow-up analyses that enable them to measure their organizational quality, identify the barriers that may be blocking change, and initiate an improvement effort based on objective data. Part of KEYS is a self-assessment tool that helps schools focus on what works, for whom, and under what conditions. Part of KEYS is a school-based improvement strategy concerned with an organization's enabling conditions and relationships, not specific programs. Finally, KEYS is a strategy to involve the NEA in school quality improvement through collegial networking, collective action, and association capacity building. This is an improvement effort that focuses on using NEA resources to lead in establishing the enabling conditions that let schools improve and students learn.

Origins of the KEYS Initiative

The NEA, which today represents over 2.6 million teachers and other education employees, has been deeply involved in improving the quality of public education since its inception in 1857. The approaches have varied, from highly academic pedagogical studies to practical self-help projects for individual classrooms, but the common goal has remained: to provide effective schooling for America's children.

During the 1980s and into the 1990s, the NEA launched numerous efforts to enhance education quality. Among them were the Mastery in Learning Project and the NEA Learning Laboratories. Mastery in Learning's primary focus was to enhance learning through school-based reform of teaching and curriculum, emphasizing the importance of making critical decisions regarding the education of children as close to the classroom as possible. The Learning Laboratories project, launched 3 years later, was dedicated to creating a network of school districts engaged in "learning" to improve learning for students and educators. It could be said that the project began to focus on the building of learning communities.

The KEYS initiative built on the NEA's long-standing tradition of innovation. KEYS was NEA's first attempt to quantify the term *school quality* and focus on student achievement. The KEYS initiative demonstrates one of many appropriate roles for teacher unions, that is, achieving conditions in schools that enable school systems and education employees to make good decisions in a knowledge-oriented society.

The Research-Based Foundation for KEYS

The NEA research that developed the KEYS initiative began with an analysis of recent research on schools as professional communities and other effective schools components. Key findings that are the building blocks for KEYS include the following:

- Collaborative work increases teachers' sense of mutual support and responsibility for effective instruction (Little, 1990; Louis, Marks, & Kruse, 1993).

- Structural conditions and human and social resources provide the foundations of professional community (Kruse & Louis, 1999).

- Maintaining commitment and finding resources for systemwide reform is difficult (Fullan, 1991).

- Professional community is enhanced by supportive leadership that focuses efforts on issues related to school improvement, collegiality, shared purpose, continuous improvement, accountability and responsibility for performance, and structural change (Bryk, Lee, & Holland, 1993; Fullan, 1991).

- For professional community to grow, teachers need additional time to work in two distinctly different ways, that is, as teaching teams and as full faculty (Louis & Kruse, 1995).

- Professional communities are defined by having five elements of practice, that is, shared values, focus on student learning, collaboration, deprivatized practice, and reflective dialogue (Kruse, Louis, & Bryk, 1995).

- In high-achieving schools, teachers report that most of their colleagues have a strong sense of responsibility for helping each other, improving the school, and setting high standards for themselves (Bryk et al., 1993).

- In low-achieving schools, there is an almost ceremonial approach to school improvement, where teachers undertake right activities but do not expect much success (Hoy, Tarter, & Rothcamp, 1991).

- School effectiveness is related to collegial, collaborative interactions among the key actors in the school (Newmann & Wehlage, 1995).

- The teachers' perceptions of the interactions between themselves and the school are an accurate reflection of the quality of the teachers' work (Hoy et al., 1991).

- An organizationally healthy school is one in which the technical, managerial, and institutional levels are in harmony (Hoy et al., 1991).

In addition, evidence from several studies of school change indicates that unless school improvement efforts truly touch the minds and hearts of teachers and become manifest in their behavior and attitudes, the ultimate aims of school reform will go unmet. On average, teachers have been teaching 17 years, working in their current district for almost 14 years, and serving in their current building for 10 years. Contrast this to the average stay of a superintendent (3 years) or even a principal (3 to 5 years) and it becomes apparent that in a long-term process like creating a quality school, teachers must play a central role.

NEA Research Supporting the KEYS Initiative

Although the development of the KEYS initiative is based on a strong foundation of research by scholars, the NEA has conducted its own research examining the relationship between organizational characteristics of schools and student learning. This research led to the development of the KEYS instrument and provides evidence that the indicators of school quality that are the focus of the KEYS assessment instrument are predictors of high student achievement. The essential findings from this research are the following:

- Quality schools are multidimensional environments, characterized by many factors that, in total, make them quality teaching and learning environments. There is no one aspect that should be the focus of policymakers in attempting to raise the quality of schools or student achievement. Although not every characteristic contributes directly to student achievement, there are indirect effects, as these characteristics are interrelated.

- Student achievement is high where school goals, mission, and objectives are clear, explicit, and continuously shared with all concerned.

- Student achievement is higher in schools where there is a shared understanding about achievable student outcomes and where there is parent and school employee commitment to long-range, continuous improvement.

- Student achievement is high where central and building administration are committed to long-range, continuous improvement.

- Student achievement is higher in schools that exhibit the belief that all students can achieve under the right conditions.

- Student achievement is higher in schools that understand and use assessment of students on a regular basis and use a variety of assessment tools.

- High-performing public schools are places where there is teacher involvement in choosing teaching materials and resources.

- High-performing schools are places where all school employees, students, parents, and the community are involved in seeking, identifying, and eliminating barriers to improvement and academic success.

- High-achieving schools are those places where employee training is based on analysis of student performance and is used to improve job performance. Emphasis is placed on developing teamwork and on improving teaching techniques.

- High-performing schools are those where continuing evaluation is focused on the system, not on individuals, and the overall quality of the school is rated.

- In high-achieving schools, two-way, nonthreatening communication is constantly occurring. Emphasis is placed on developing a climate for innovation.

- In high-achieving schools, there is concern for the appropriate and cautious use of standardized tests. Multiple forms of assessment are used to identify needs for and strategies of improvement.

In short, an impressive amount of important theory, research, and practice leads one to the conclusion that the structural and organizational features of schools affect the conditions of teaching and learning and, in turn, these conditions significantly influence student achievement.

Guidelines for School Improvement

Research by the NEA and others provide several guidelines for actions that provide direction for schools that wish to increase their quality:

- Strive for shared understanding about achievable education outcomes. Work collaboratively to define a purpose and goals and to determine quantifiable outcomes along with the best methods, strategies, and actions to achieve those outcomes.

- Involve the total learning community—all stakeholders, teachers, education support personnel, administrators, parents, and community and business organizations—in quality improvement planning and problem-solving the implementation of necessary changes.

- Engage in continuous, ongoing assessment of teaching and learning and base decision making on this assessment. Establish accountability at all levels to ensure consistent application of the study's principles.

- Emphasize personal and professional learning and development. Create a learning environment for the organization. Establish regular, needs-specific staff development focused on solving problems related to student needs to educate and retrain employees. Professional development for teachers and administrators should be an integral part of any plan to decentralize management practices. As much as possible, this training should be designed to meet the needs of students in individual schools.

- Don't play the quality game unless you are willing to keep score. Be ready to show quantifiable "before and after" data on your change efforts. Focus on assessing the system and its programs rather than on individuals.

- Build two-way, nonthreatening communication channels among all stakeholders.

- Frequently clarify the expectations, purpose, and progress related to school improvement for the entire learning community.

- Ensure that materials and social support for continuous improvement are provided.

Conclusion

Many of those who would reform our schools continue to seek straightforward, simple, and inexpensive recipes for what works in schools. All too often, they neglect vital organizational and cultural characteristics of schools that affect student outcomes. The chapters in this book argue that any comprehensive approach to educational improvement needs to address the challenges involved in creating and sustaining conditions in schools that fundamentally influence the quality of teaching and thereby the opportunities students have to achieve at high levels.

References

Bryk, A. S., Lee, V., & Holland, P. (1993). *Catholic schools and the common good.* Cambridge, MA: Harvard University Press.

Fullan, M. (1991). *The new meaning of educational change.* New York: Teachers College Press.

Hoy, W. K., Tarter, C. J., & Rothcamp, R. B. (1991). *Open schools, healthy schools: Measuring organizational climate.* Newbury Park, CA: Sage.

Kruse, S. D., & Louis, K. S. (1999). Creating community in reform: Images of organizational learning in urban schools. In K. Leithwood & K. S. Louis (Eds.), *Organizational learning and school improvement: Linkages and strategies.* Lisse, The Netherlands: Swets & Zeitlinger.

Kruse, S. D., Louis, K. L., & Bryk, A. S. (1995). An emerging framework for analyzing school-based professional community. In K. S. Louis & S. D. Kruse (Eds.), *Professionalism and community: Perspectives on urban educational reform.* Thousand Oaks, CA: Corwin.

Little, J. W. (1990). The persistence of privacy: Autonomy and interaction in professional relations. *Teachers College Record, 91*(4), 509-536.

Louis, K. S., & Kruse, S. D. (1995). *Professionalism and community: Perspectives on urban educational reform.* Thousand Oaks, CA: Corwin.

Louis, K. S., Marks, H., & Kruse, S. D. (1993). Schoolwide professional community. *American Educational Research Journal, 33*(3), 719-752.

Newmann, F. M., & Wehlage, G. G. (1995). *Successful school restructuring: A report to the public and educators.* Madison: Center on Organization and Restructuring of Schools, Wisconsin Center for Education Research, University of Wisconsin.

About the Editors

Willis D. Hawley is Professor of Education and Public Affairs at the University of Maryland, where he served as Dean of the College of Education from 1993 to 1998. He taught at Yale, Duke, and Vanderbilt universities before going to Maryland. He has published numerous books, articles, and book chapters dealing with teacher education, school reform, urban politics, political learning, organizational change, school desegregation, and educational policy. His most recent research deals with the professional development of teachers, the education of teachers (in the United States and Japan), school restructuring and effectiveness, family influences on the academic performance of Southeast Asian children in the United States, and race relations. He has served as consultant to numerous public agencies, including the Executive Office of the President, the U.S. Senate, the U.S. Department of Education, and the World Bank, as well as many state and local governments, foundations, and professional associations. He also organized and directs the Common Destiny Alliance, a coalition of national organizations and scholars interested in using research to improve intergroup relations.

Donald L. Rollie is Manager of Quality Schools, Research and Policy, for the National Education Association (NEA). He is also the President and Chief Executive Officer of Donald L. Rollie and Associates, a consulting group that combines the expertise of veteran educators and organizational development specialists. Rollie himself is both. His current work with the Teaching and Learning unit of the NEA is an important part of the NEA journey on the path of change, returning to becoming a voice for education quality in America.

About the Contributors

Patricia A. Alexander is Professor and Distinguished Scholar/Teacher in the Department of Human Development at the University of Maryland. Her research addresses such topics as learning; individual differences; and the interaction of knowledge, interest, and strategic processing. Her recent publications have focused on the nature of academic development, particularly as it relates to domain-specific knowledge and to learning from text.

Eva L. Baker is Professor in UCLA's Graduate School of Education and Information Studies, and Co-Director of the National Center for Research on Evaluation, Standards, and Student Testing at UCLA. Her research focuses on the design and validation of technology-based learning and assessment systems and on new models to measure complex human performance in large-scale assessments. She cochaired the Joint Committee on the Revision of the Standards for Educational and Psychological Testing in 1999 and currently chairs the National Academy of Sciences' Board on Testing and Assessment.

Lorna M. Earl is Associate Professor in the Theory and Policy Studies Department and Co-Director of the International Centre for Educational Change at the Ontario Institute for Studies in Education, University of Toronto. She is a leader in the field of assessment and evaluation and has been involved in consultation, research, and staff development with teachers' organizations, ministries of education, school boards, and charitable foundations throughout the world. The author of many articles and monographs on a wide variety of educational issues, her primary interest is the wise application of research, assessment, and evaluation knowledge to the realities of schools and classrooms and to policy decisions.

Richard F. Elmore is Professor of Education at Harvard University and a Senior Research Fellow with the Consortium for Policy Research in Education (CPRE), funded by the U.S. Department of Education's Office of Educational Research and Improvement. He is currently Co-Director, with Leslie

Santee Siskin, of a CPRE research project on school accountability. He is also Co-Principal Investigator of a multiyear study of instructional improvement and professional development in Community School District 2, New York City, with Lauren Resnick and Anthony Alvorado, funded by OERI/ED through the Learning Research and Development Center at the University of Pittsburgh. His most recent publications include *Restructuring in the Classroom* (coauthored with Penelope Peterson and Sarah McCarthey), "Getting to Scale with Good Educational Practice," and "Investing in Teacher Learning: Staff Development and Instructional Improvement in Community School District #2, New York City."

Michael Fullan is Dean of the Ontario Institute for Studies in Education (OISE) of the University of Toronto. An innovator and leader in teacher education, he has developed a number of partnerships designed to bring about major school improvement and educational reform. He participates as researcher, consultant, trainer, and policy advisor on a wide range of educational change projects with school systems, teachers' federations, research and development institutes, and government agencies in Canada and internationally. He has published widely on the topic of educational change. His most recent books are *Change Forces: The Sequel*, *Change Forces: Probing the Depths of Educational Reform*, the *What's Worth Fighting For* series, and *The New Meaning of Educational Change*. He has received numerous awards, including the Colonel Watson Award for Outstanding Leadership, the Canadian Education Association's Whitworth Award for Educational Research, and the Branco Weiss Award for Outstanding Contribution to the Development of Thinking in Education.

Kenneth Leithwood is Professor of Educational Administration, and Director of the Centre for Leadership Development at the University of Toronto (OISE). His research and writing about school leadership and organizational change are widely known and respected by educators throughout the English-speaking world. He is the senior editor of the recent *International Handbook on Educational Leadership and Administration*. Some of his other recent books include *Understanding Schools As Intelligent Systems*, *Changing Leadership for Changing Times*, *Organizational Learning in Schools* (with Karen Seashore Louis), *Expert Problem Solving: Evidence From School and District Leaders*, and *Making Schools Smarter* (Corwin Press, 1995). He is responsible for the design and implementation of school leadership development programs at the University of Toronto (OISE) and consults with many other leadership development agencies as well; for example, he is currently the external evaluator of the Greater New Orleans School Leadership Center.

Ann Lieberman is Emeritus Professor from Teachers College, Columbia University. She is now Senior Scholar at the Carnegie Foundation for the Advancement of Teaching and Visiting Professor at Stanford University. She was president of the American Educational Research Association (AERA) in 1992. She is widely known for her work in the areas of teacher leadership and development; collaborative research; networks and school-university partnerships; and, increasingly, the problems and prospects of educational change.

Judith Warren Little is Professor at the Graduate School of Education, University of California, Berkeley. A sociologist by training, she concentrates her research on teachers' work, professional development, and the contexts of teaching. She has published numerous articles and coedited two books on teachers' work and professional relationships. For the past several years, she has been studying the conditions of teaching and reform in California high schools. Her most recent book is *The Subjects in Question: Departmental Organization and the High School* (with Leslie Siskin).

Lynne Miller is Professor of Educational Leadership and Director of the Southern Maine Partnership at the University of Southern Maine. She previously served as a high school English teacher, alternative school director, and building and district administrator. She was a member of the National Commission on Teaching and America's Future and remains active in regional and national discussions about teacher quality. She has written widely in the areas of teacher development, school renewal, and the realities of school reform.

P. Karen Murphy is Assistant Professor of Educational Psychology in the College of Education at The Ohio State University, Columbus. She is interested in the processes underpinning students' learning and how cognition and motivation impact these processes. Her current research projects pertain to the impact of students' and teachers' knowledge, beliefs, and interest on learning; student learning in particular domains; the impact of technology in classroom learning; and the linking of philosophy and psychology in educational psychology.

Fred M. Newmann, Emeritus Professor of Curriculum and Instruction, University of Wisconsin–Madison, directed the National Center on Effective

Secondary Schools and the Center on Organization and Restructuring of Schools. With 30 years' experience in school reform research, curriculum development, and teacher education, he contributed new curriculum in the analysis of public controversy and community-based learning. His research has addressed higher-order thinking in social studies, student engagement in secondary schools, authentic achievement and assessment, and professional development to build capacity in low-income schools.

Linda Valli is Associate Professor of Education in the Department of Curriculum and Instruction at the University of Maryland, College Park. She has also been a junior and senior high school teacher, a director of teacher education, and an associate dean. Her research interests include teacher preparation, professional development, school improvement, and cultural diversity. She has published numerous book chapters as well as articles in such journals as *Teaching and Teacher Education, Journal of Teacher Education,* and *Action in Teacher Education,* and has authored or edited three books, including *Reflective Teacher Education: Cases and Critiques.*

This book is dedicated to the memory of
Oscar Uribe, Jr., a champion of the KEYS initiative

CHAPTER 1

Educational Reform as Continuous Improvement

Michael Fullan
Ontario Institute for Studies in Education
University of Toronto

The chapters in this book were prepared to serve as a resource document for the National Education Association's (NEA; 1997) KEYS project. KEYS is an acronym for Keys to Excellence in Your Schools. NEA has identified numerous factors essential to effective schools, and has developed a survey instrument designed to gather data on these items and in turn to feed back the data to participating schools. The items cluster into six main domains:

- Knowledge of teaching and learning
- Shared understanding and commitment to high goals
- Open communication and collaborative problem solving
- Continuous assessment for teaching and learning
- Personal and professional learning
- Resources to support teaching and learning

The KEYS project is one example of the larger effort to transform the teaching profession. The National Commission on Teaching and America's Future (NCTAF; 1996) documented the problem:

1. Low expectations for student performance

2. Unenforced standards for teachers

3. Major flaws in teacher preparation

4. Painfully slipshod teacher recruitment

5. Inadequate induction for beginning teachers

6. Lack of professional development and rewards for knowledge and skill

7. Schools that are structured for failure rather than success (p. 24)

This is not the first time that the reform of teaching has come to the forefront of concerns about improving schools (Fullan, Galluzzo, Morris, & Watson, 1998).

What is needed, as my colleagues and I argued in our study, *The Rise and Stall of Teacher Education Reform,* is a comprehensive sustained initiative that incorporates the following:

- A stronger knowledge base for teaching and teacher education
- Attracting able, diverse, and committed students to the career of teaching
- Redesigning teacher preparation programs so that the links to arts and sciences and to the field of practice are both strengthened
- Reform in the working conditions of schools
- The development and monitoring of external standards for progress as well as for teacher candidates and teachers on the job
- A rigorous and dynamic research enterprise focusing on teaching, teacher education, and the assessment and monitoring of strategies (Fullan et al., 1998, p. 58)

We have also said that teachers, ranging from the individual teacher in the classroom to the most visible union leader, must "help to recreate the profession." Hargreaves and I concluded in *What's Worth Fighting For Out There* (1998) that the teaching profession has not yet come of age and that the next decade

> will be defining era for teaching profession. Will it become a stronger learning profession? Will it become a force for societal change and social practice? Can it develop its own visions of and commitments to educational and social change, instead of simply vetoing and reacting to the change agendas of others? (p. 103)

The KEYS project—with its survey instrument, feedback, action planning, and on-line professional development in the schools and districts participating in the program—is engaged in very difficult work. The ultimate goal is to mobilize thousands of schools and districts in transforming professional development and organizational learning. The KEYS project by itself will not accomplish such fundamental reform. It can, however, have a significant impact if it connects the powerful concepts in the KEYS instrument with the content priorities embedded in the new teaching and learning curriculum being developed across the nation. In short, systematic professional development, focused on teaching and learning, learning schools and school districts, and success for all students are closely intertwined.

What we need, then, is to consolidate the knowledge base about what makes for continuous improvement, and correspondingly to mobilize sets of actions among educators in partnership with others to engage in reform initiatives that are based on this knowledge base.

The chapters in the book were prepared to serve as a resource document for the KEYS project. The chapters align with the themes as follows:

- Knowledge of teaching and learning—Murphy and Alexander
- Shared understanding and commitment—Newmann
- Communication and problem solving—Little
- Assessment for teaching and learning—Baker; Earl
- Personal and professional learning—Lieberman and Miller; Valli and Hawley
- Resources—Leithwood; Elmore

The assumption of KEYS is that schools and districts that focus on the six clusters, and do so in a way that connects these themes closely to particular curriculum priorities, will increase their capacity to achieve coherence and focus and will affect learning for all students in the system.

In this introductory chapter, I start with the core argument that professional development, pedagogical improvement, and student learning need to be tightly interwoven for schools to be effective. The Newmann, Little, Baker, and Earl chapters form the basis of this conclusion. Murphy and Alexander summarize research that identifies essential knowledge about student learning.

Second, I reinforce the argument by examining personal and professional learning. These ideas are founded on the chapters by Lieberman and Miller and Valli and Hawley.

Third, you can't have learning organizations without having schools and districts as learning systems and without having teaching as a learning profession. The last section focuses on schools and districts as learning systems and on teaching as a profession. Leithwood and Elmore provide analyses that show how districts need to become involved in continuous learning. Although much has been accomplished over the past several years in clarifying and demonstrating effective professional development, the more fundamental issue is the evolution of teaching as a professional development. I see the KEYS project in the context of the changing teaching profession.

Deep Understanding of How People Learn

The fundamental goal of school improvement is, of course, improved student learning. Quality teaching is the key determinant of student learning. In the past several years, research on learning has significantly altered the traditional understanding of how people learn, and this research is changing the definition of high-quality teaching. Murphy and Alexander were commissioned by the American Psychological Association to synthesize and summarize research on learning and to identify implications of this research for how we think about teaching. Chapter 2, their chapter in this book, provides a succinct but authoritative review of research on teaching and learning that is relevant to the development of strategies to restructure schools as learning organizations for both students and teachers.

Professional Community, Pedagogical Improvement, and Student Learning

In Chapter 3, Newmann makes the case—strongly backed up by research he and his colleagues conducted—that three core things must come together in a highly interactive and systematic way if a school is to become effective. First, there must be a professional learning community in which teachers and others develop (as a result of continuous interaction) shared understanding and commitment to achieve high-level outcomes for all students. Second, this joint work must focus on critically assessing and adopting new instructional practices that are best suited for accomplishing high-level outcomes for all students. Third, and in turn, shared understanding and new teaching techniques must be determined by what students are learning. In brief, these three factors—professional community, instructional practice, and assessment of student work—feed on each other to create new synergies tantamount to continuous improvement.

In Chapter 4, Little establishes the theoretical underpinning in relation to Newmann's findings on shared understanding. Little indicates why professional development, communication, and collaboration must go together, and in so doing shows how this cluster affects the "culture" of professional relationships. Hargreaves and I have called this the need to *reculture* the school away from isolating, balkanized, and superficial collegiality toward strong forms of collaboration (Fullan & Hargreaves, 1996; Hargreaves & Fullan, 1998). Similarly, Little talks about three supporting conditions for culture building: (a) shared interests and shared responsibility, (b) opportunity to interact and learn, and (c) resources. Little concludes with a point that we will return to in the last section—that collaboration does not mean agreement and does not mean absence of conflict. As I shall argue later, the more that people collaborate the more that they have to disagree about.

Until recently, student assessment was not carefully examined in the work on collaborative cultures. It now becomes clear, as Baker (Chapter 5) and Earl (Chapter 6) demonstrate, that assessment of student work and corresponding planning for improvement are essential for school effectiveness.

Baker takes up the issue of "improving the learning of students who are tested" by involving students in reflecting on their work and by engaging teachers in altering their teaching to help students reach academic goals. Earl extends these ideas by claiming "classroom assessment can be one of the most powerful levers for enforcing student learning." As Earl concludes:

> When teachers share the decisions about how to assess, there will be fewer discrepancies in student assessment standards and procedures between grades or classes; they will develop a deeper understanding of curriculum and of individual students; and they will engage in the intense discussions about standards and evidence that lead to a shared understanding of expectations for students, more refined language about children and learning, and consistent procedures for making and communicating judgments.

As Hargreaves and I have also said, teachers must become "assessment literate" for two reasons (Hargreaves & Fullan, 1998). First, external assessment and accountability are here to stay. The "out there" is now "in here," and educators need to "move toward the danger" and learn to hold their own in the politically contentious arena of debating how well students are doing. Second, becoming assessment literate is absolutely essential for examining and improving one's own teaching practices to get better results. Examining student work with other teachers is a powerful strategy for enhancing teaching and learning. Thus professional learning community, instructional practices, and student learning go hand in hand.

Personal and Professional Learning

Lieberman and Miller conclude in Chapter 7 that professional development must be transformed to encompass (a) teacher career development, (b) organizing schools to support ongoing learning communities, and (c) education reform networks that support teacher learning. Thus personal learning, organizational (school-based) learning, and broader education reform networks (subject matter collaborative, school-university partnerships, and other reform networks) are all playing a role in building new learning communities and reshaping professional development.

Valli and Hawley in Chapter 8 consolidate learning about professional development in nine basic principles or "essentials" of effective teacher learning:

1. Professional development should focus on specific strategies for teaching the content students are expected to learn.

2. Professional development should be driven by analyses of the differences between (a) goals and standards for student learning, and (b) student performance.

3. Professional development should involve teachers in the identification of what they need to learn and, when possible, in the development of the learning opportunity or the process to be used.

4. Professional development should be primarily school based and integral to school operations.

5. Professional development should provide learning opportunities that relate to individual needs but are for the most part organized around collaborative problem solving.

6. Professional development should be continuous and ongoing, involving follow-up and support for further learning—including support from sources external to the school that can provide necessary resources and an outside perspective.

7. Professional development should incorporate evaluation of multiple sources of information on (a) outcomes for students, and (b) processes that are involved in implementing the lessons learned through professional development.

8. Professional development should provide opportunities to engage in developing a theoretical understanding of the knowledge and skills to be learned.

9. Professional development should be integrated with a comprehensive change process that deals with impediments to and facilitators of student learning.

These essential principles, of course, are entirely compatible with and reinforcing of the other chapters in this book and represent a solid summary of the knowledge base for effective professional development.

The School and District as Learning Organizations

A great deal of lip service is given to the concept of learning organizations, but what does it really mean in concrete terms? At the general level, it means continually acquiring new knowledge, skills, and understanding to improve one's actions and results. Thus when professional development, collaboration, pedagogical improvement, and student learning interact over time, organizational learning is occurring at the school level.

The challenge is to do for entire school districts what Newmann and our other authors have done for individual schools, namely, establish systemwide frameworks of accountability, support teachers and others in analyzing their instructional practices together in light of what students are learning, and establish processes of continuous learning in and across schools. This is something that has not normally happened. There are, however, several examples in the literature of successful attempts at turning school districts into learning organizations, including Elmore's (1996) study of District 2 in New York City, the four urban districts in the Rockefeller Foundation's professional development infrastructure initiative (Fullan, Watson, & Kilcher, 1997), and the Durham School District in Ontario, Canada (Fullan, Alberts, Lieberman, & Zywine, 1996). It is only recently that districtwide improvement has been the focus of reform strategies and corresponding research; so much more needs to be done in this domain. In Chapter 9, Leithwood maps out what has to be done at the system level to create learning schools and districts. He describes seven sets of conditions that enhance the likelihood of organizational learning in schools. These conditions are related to mission and goals, culture, structure and organization, information-collection and decision-making processes, policies and procedures, school-community partnerships, and leadership.

In Chapter 10, Elmore raises the question of how entire school districts—large sets of schools—can become learning systems. He does this in a way that is founded on the ideas in the chapters reviewed so far. As he puts it, "The single most persistent problem of educational reform in the United States is the failure of reforms to alter the fundamental conditions of teaching and learning for students and teachers in schools in anything other than a small-scale and idiosyncratic way."

Summary

In summary, there are new developments in the field of educational reform that are based on two interrelated forces. One is the knowledge base, which more and more specifically characterizes what makes for continuous improvement in schools and school systems; the other is the increasing commitment to achieve reform on a larger scale. In the next few years, we expect to see more and more large-scale reform initiatives that build on this knowledge base (see also Fullan, 1999).

References and Resources

Elmore, R. (1996). *Staff development and instructional improvement in Community School District #2, New York City.* Cambridge, MA: Consortium for Policy Research in Education, Harvard University.

Fullan, M. (1999). *Change forces: The sequel.* Philadelphia: Falmer.

Fullan, M., Alberts, B., Lieberman, A., & Zywine, J. (1996). *Report of Country Expert Commission Canada/United States of America.* Carl Bertelsmann Prize.

Fullan, M., Galluzzo, G., Morris, P., & Watson, N. (1998). *The rise and stall of teacher education reform.* Washington, DC: American Association of Colleges for Teacher Education.

Fullan, M., & Hargreaves, A. (1996). *What's worth fighting for in your school.* New York: Teachers College Press.

Fullan, M., Watson, N., & Kilcher, A. (1997). *Building infrastructures for professional development.* New York: Rockefeller Foundation.

Hargreaves, A., & Fullan, M. (1998). *What's worth fighting for out there.* New York: Teachers' College Press.

National Commission on Teaching and America's Future. (1996). *What matters most: Teaching for America's future.* Washington, DC: Author.

National Education Association. (1997). *Keys Project: Study and implementation of quality conditions of teaching and learning.* Washington, DC: Author.

CHAPTER

The Learner-Centered Principles
Their Value for Teachers and Teaching

P. Karen Murphy
The Ohio State University

Patricia A. Alexander
University of Maryland

It seems that each new decade comes with its own set of educational reform initiatives. These initiatives arise from internal sources (e.g., teachers or school administrators) as well as from external constituents (e.g., parents and policymakers). In just the latter half of the 20th century, for example, reform efforts produced alternative conceptualizations of teachers as knowledge transmitters, scientists, and technicians and of teaching as scaffolding, apprenticing, and shared participation (e.g., Palincsar & Brown, 1984; Rogoff, 1990). Such initiatives serve to capture the prevailing philosophical orientations toward teaching as well as signal developing trends in research and practices of the time. More often than not, however, these initiatives are short-lived. As a result, very few teaching or learning initiatives are around long enough to produce broad and durable outcomes (Alexander, Murphy, & Woods, 1996).

Perhaps one of the most significant calls for educational reform in the past two decades was *A Nation at Risk,* the report of the National Commission on Excellence in Education, published in 1983 by the U.S. Department of Education. Six years later, this report was followed by a summit meeting of the nation's governors and former President Bush. The outcomes of this summit highlighted national concerns about education and what would be needed to improve the current educational system. In response to this call, the American Psychological Association (APA) appointed a task force of experts in psychology and education with the charge of developing a framework of principles based on the field's understanding of what promotes optimal learning (APA Presidential Task Force on Psychology in Education, 1993). The 12 original principles that emerged from this initial task force were subsequently revised and expanded by another APA task force based on suggestions and revisions from major scientific societies, psychological organizations, and professional educational associations (APA Board of Educational Affairs, 1995). These final 14 principles, representing a synthesis of what is known about learners and optimal learning from a psychological perspective, were conceived as a framework for guiding educational practice.

Prior to discussing the principles and their value for teachers and teaching, it seems imperative to explain the notion of *learner centered* as conceptualized in the APA document. Intuitively, this term seems to describe a classroom in which activities are focused around the needs of the learner and in which the teacher plays the role of facilitator. Such an understanding is reminiscent of child- or student-centered philosophies associated with preschool and early childhood education (Lambert & McCombs, 1998). As Lambert and McCombs suggested, however, the *learner-centered principles* extend far beyond the artificial boundaries of formal schooling: "The principles apply to all of us, cradle to grave, from students in the classroom to teachers, administrators, parents, and others influenced by the process of schooling" (p. 9). An extremely comprehensive definition of *learner centered* has been offered by McCombs and Whisler (1997):

> The perspective that couples a focus on individual learners (their heredity, experiences, perspectives, backgrounds, talents, interests, capacities, and needs) with a focus on learning (the best available knowledge about learning and how it occurs and about teaching practices that are most effective in promoting the highest levels of motivation, learning, and achievement for all learners). This dual focus, then, informs and drives educational decision making. (p. 9)

The overarching value of the learner-centered principles for teachers and teaching is that they are focused both on the individual student (e.g., background experiences, culture, and needs) and on what psychological research reveals about optimal learning. Since the principles are rooted deeply in psychological research, they provide educators with a valid mechanism for understanding students and the processes that undergird educational change. As a result, the principles have been promoted for contributing to meaningful and enduring school reform. Because of their precise attention to the nature of learning from both an individual and a collective perspective, we believe that a thorough knowledge of the principles can be an effective catalyst for systemic change. We believe such rooted reform will be far more likely to improve schools than the rather trendy and sometimes questionable reforms of the past (Alexander et al., 1996).

Furthermore, given their broad and comprehensive scope, these learner-centered principles can be beneficial to teachers, teaching, and schools for other reasons. For instance, the principles can foster professional development (Valli & Hawley, Chapter 8, this volume). The learner-centered principles offer teachers a psychological portrait of students and the processes that stimulate or stifle their learning. Teachers can compare their own personal knowledge and competencies against this psychological framework. Subsequent professional development activities can then be planned to meet the needs of the individual or the collective. Regrettably, however, many preservice and inservice teachers receive very little formal training in such psychological dimensions of learners and learning (Alexander, Murphy, & Woods, 1997), suggesting a great need for professional development in these areas.

We have chosen to focus on five extremely important themes contained in these principles rather than to discuss each of the 14 individual items specified in the APA document. We hold that parsed down to their fundamental roots, the learner-centered principles relate to five essential dimensions of meaningful learning. These dimensions, extensively investigated in psychology and related disciplines, fall under the following headings: (a) the knowledge base, (b) motivation or affect, (c) strategic processing or executive control, (d) development and individual differences, and (e) situation or context. For each of these five areas, we consider key findings from the educational research ("What We Know"), along with implications for teachers and teaching ("What It Means"). A summary of these research findings and educational implications appears in Table 2.1.

The Knowledge Base

One's existing knowledge serves as the foundation of all future learning by guiding organization and representations, by serving as a basis of association with new information, and by coloring and filtering all new experiences.

Table 2.1 Research Underlying the Various Dimensions of the Learner-Centered Principles and Its Implications for Teachers and Teaching

Research Findings	Educational Implications
THE KNOWLEDGE BASE	
• Prior knowledge predicts future learning. • Knowledge is multifaceted and multidimensional. • Knowledge misconceptions can deter or interfere with future growth.	• It is important to have a firm grasp of what students know and believe, and use that knowledge as an instructional bridge. • Learning tasks should be structured so that students understand the *what, how,* and *when.* • It is best to provide experiences that enable students to correct or modify their misunderstandings prior to teaching new content.
MOTIVATION AND AFFECT	
• Intrinsic motivation and personal interest lead to greater achievement. • Learning is enhanced when students' goals are focused on learning and mastery of content rather than performance. • Students' beliefs about their ability to complete a task are at least as important as their actual ability.	• It is important to structure activities that will tap students' deep-seated interests. • Permitted choice and a sense of agency in learning tasks, students will likely perform better on learning tasks. • It is important to structure incremental activities that allow students to build their abilities as well as their beliefs about how well they can perform.
STRATEGIC PROCESSING OR EXECUTIVE CONTROL	
• Learning is enhanced when students use cognitive and metacognitive strategies.	• Students must be taught how to think reflectively about their learning and performance.

(continued)

Table 2.1 Continued

Research Findings	Educational Implications
• Strategic processing and executive control are influenced by the novelty of the task or situation. • Strategic processing is by definition both purposeful and effortful.	• Training in strategic processing should be regularly linked to new tasks and new situations. • An environment should be created that rewards and encourages strategic processing.

DEVELOPMENT AND INDIVIDUAL DIFFERENCES

• There are predictable and defined global patterns in human development. • Individuals retain their uniqueness. • Individual learner differences can both help and hinder the learning process. • Both heredity and environment influence development and individual differences.	• Not every child in a particular classroom should be expected to be at the same developmental level. • Individual differences should be embraced and students helped to use their individual differences to enhance individuality in learning. • It should be recognized that a student's heredity and experiential factors both contribute to who that student is as a learner.

SITUATION OR CONTEXT

• The social context is an influential factor in learning. • All learning is filtered through one's sociocultural context and knowledge. • Teachers are vital components in facilitating and guiding the social exchanges that take place in classrooms.	• Classrooms should encourage both individual and social learning and growth. • Activities should be considered that explore and challenge the context through which students view learning. • Direct and individual assistance in student learning should be provided.

What We Know

One of the most powerful and consistent findings to emerge from cognitive research over the past several decades pertains to the power of the knowledge base (i.e., the total of all an individual knows or believes) on learning (Alexander, Schallert, & Hare, 1991). That is, the knowledge base is an extremely strong force that directs students' attention, colors their judgments about what is relevant or important, impacts their comprehension and memory, and shapes the way they perceive their world (e.g., Reynolds & Shirey, 1988). Truly a student's prior experiences, beliefs, and knowledge serve as the scaffold that supports the construction of future knowledge. From this perspective, knowledge has come to be viewed as a multifaceted construct that encompasses many interactive dimensions (e.g., sociocultural knowledge, domain knowledge, or personal beliefs). For example, Lipson (1983) examined how students' religious orientations influenced the way they comprehended and recalled passages about religious practices. Similarly, Chambliss and Garner (1996) investigated how adults' views on logging practices in the western United States altered their reading of persuasive texts. Knowledge is also multidimensional in that there are several states (i.e., declarative, procedural, and conditional) and multiple forms of knowledge (e.g., in-school knowledge and out-of-school knowledge). By declarative knowledge, we mean the more factual understanding or *knowing what* or *knowing that.* Procedural knowledge, by comparison, refers to *knowing how* to do something (Alexander et al., 1991). Conditional knowledge pertains to understanding *when* or *where* to apply one's knowledge. In addition, students' knowledge can sometimes remain buried in memory or be seriously flawed or misleading (e.g., Chinn & Brewer, 1993). Therefore, although knowledge is generally a positive force in learning, there are times when this will not be the case. If learners operate on incomplete and inaccurate knowledge, their existing misconceptions can actually deter or interfere with future growth.

What It Means

Each student constructs knowledge in accordance with his or her past experiences. Thus it is extremely important that teachers use various forms of formal and informal assessments to gauge what students know or believe to be true. This understanding can then be used as a scaffold for future lessons and learning tasks. For example, a teacher might use students' current understandings about the rising and setting of the sun as a beginning point for a lesson on the earth's rotation. In addition, educators should strive to structure activities so that the various states or forms of knowledge are explored. For example, a biology teacher teaching the parts of the cell may have students play the role of individual components in the cell. In doing so, students would also learn both the *whats* and the *hows* of cell functioning. One benefit of such hands-on instruction in the sciences is its promotion of multiple forms of knowing (e.g., Gardner, 1993). Finally, teachers must be aware of the naïve understandings or misconceptions that students may hold in an area of study. Armed with this knowledge, teachers can confront their students' underdeveloped or malformed notions in the context of instruction.

In many cases, students will base their conceptions of scientific processes on their out-of-school experiences. As a case in point, many students think that watering a lawn keeps the lawn green, when in fact photosynthesis is the scientific process that makes grass and other plants green. Instead of just teaching about photosynthesis, teachers might have the students conduct an experiment that would counter their naïve understandings. By doing so, teachers will help students construct a richer and more accurate knowledge base that will enable future learning.

Motivation and Affect

Motivational or affective factors, such as intrinsic motivation, personal goals, attributions for learning, and self-efficacy, along with the motivational characteristics of learning tasks, play a significant role in the learning process.

What We Know

As is evident to most teachers, learning is altered by motivational and affective factors in the learner and in the learning environment. Indeed, the research on motivation and affect has documented that personal interest, intrinsic motivation, and internal commitment contribute to greater learning (e.g., Ames & Ames, 1989). That is, topics or areas of study that students possess a deep-seated interest in or are internally motivated to pursue will likely relate to higher achievement. Similarly, those learners who have goals of pursuing understanding (i.e., mastery or learning goals) rather than performing for external rewards or recognition are more apt to achieve in schools (e.g., Murphy & Alexander, 2000). In particular, when students set their sights on learning for its own sake rather than to gain acclaim or rewards they are more apt to achieve competence (Alexander, 1997).

Finally, students with strong self-efficacy beliefs (i.e., beliefs that one can achieve a particular task outcome) are more likely to succeed in schools (e.g., Bandura, 1986). That is, research would suggest that students' beliefs about their ability to achieve some goal or execute some task-related activity are at least as influential in learning outcomes as their actual abilities. At the same time, learners are apt to show higher levels of motivation (e.g., interest or involvement) for some fields of study compared to others and for certain tasks but not for others (e.g., Alexander, Kulikowich, & Schulze, 1994). In sum, it would seem that the application of the literatures in motivation and affect to the reshaping and reformation of the educational system will need to consider not only learners' general needs, desires, self-perceptions, and emotional states or orientations but also their specific interests, goals, and desires.

What It Means

Essentially, students are driven or motivated by their deep-seated interests. When tasks or learning outcomes parallel those interests, students achieve. Thus the classroom environment in which students operate plays a significant role in learning. Therefore teachers should acknowledge students' goals and interests and cultivate an academic climate that is supportive and encouraging of students' individual interests and goals to the extent that students' goals further the desired instructional goals.

Student choice and self-determination can also enhance motivation. For example, a teacher instructing students on ecosystems might allow students to choose the type of ecosystem they would like to study. Then the teacher can draw similarities across the various ecosystems studied by the students. One caveat about motivation, however, is that no student is equally motivated in all areas of study. That is, teachers should understand that no student is highly and consistently engaged in academic pursuits. Although there are a number of reasons for students' lack of motivation, teachers should recognize that students are often unmotivated about tasks or subjects in which they believe they will not succeed. To overcome such beliefs, teachers can structure incremental activities that allow students to build their abilities, and these small successes will enable students to believe in their ability to achieve.

Strategic Processing or Executive Control

The ability to reflect on and regulate one's thoughts and behaviors is essential to learning and development.

What We Know

Effective learners not only possess a body of organized and relevant knowledge, but they also have the ability and willingness to direct, reflect on, and oversee their own mental functioning and to assess their own performance (McCombs, 1998). Studies have consistently demonstrated that learning is enhanced when individuals have knowledge of and apply appropriate cognitive and metacognitive or self-regulatory strategies during the learning process (e.g., Garner & Alexander, 1989). Essentially, those who reflect on their own thinking and learning performance and use that self-knowledge to alter their processing are more likely to manifest significant academic growth than those who do not. Students' use of self-monitoring strategies, however, is highly dependent on the educational situation or context (Garner 1990). For example, successful students may choose to monitor tasks they perceive as difficult, whereas less successful students may choose to do very little monitoring or regulating on the same tasks. Indeed, the reflection and strategic efforts must, almost by definition, vary as the demands of the task or the nature of the context changes (e.g., Lave, 1988; Resnick, 1991).

To assume that one can simply have students memorize and routinely execute a set of strategies is to misconceive the nature of strategic processing or executive control. Such rote applications of these procedures represent, in essence, a *nonstrategic* approach to strategic processing. It has become increasingly clear as well that strategic processing or executive control is not only a purposeful undertaking but also an effortful one (Borkowski, Carr, & Pressley, 1987). This means that it is difficult to bring about changes in students' strategic processing without addressing issues of motivation, interest, and self-regulation (Alexander, 1997).

What It Means

Students rarely come to school with a repertoire of strategies for performing school-based tasks. Thus students must be taught how to monitor their own mental processing. Furthermore, students should be shown how particular strategies are most effectively applied to particular activities. In addition, teachers should realize that training in strategic processing must be broad in scope and extended over time if there is to be any hope that those strategic processes will transfer to new tasks or situations. To aid in this transfer, teachers will want to apply new strategies to routine tasks and routine strategies to novel tasks. Moreover, because strategic thinking takes time and energy, teachers must build into their plans sufficient time for reflection and the use of appropriate incentives (Garner, 1990). By creating an environment that rewards and encourages strategic processing under varying conditions, teachers can help students see that the time and effort required for strategic behavior is justified. Teachers who make strategic processing an explicit and valued component in instruction and who orchestrate and maintain such a challenging but supportive learning environment can expect their efforts to translate into greater learning gains for their students.

Development and Individual Differences

Learning, although ultimately a unique adventure for all, progresses through various common stages of development influenced by both inherited and experiential or environmental factors.

What We Know

An important transition in research on human development and individual differences is the recognition that learning is characterized by the continual interplay between the *nomothetic* (generalizable) and *idiographic* (individualistic) components of human development. In other words, human learning and growth are a continuous interchange between the generalizable patterns that give human thoughts and actions their predictability and individualistic characteristics and behaviors that are inevitable. Indeed, whether the focus is on cognitive, socioemotional, or moral domains, educators must have knowledge of common benchmarks of human development (e.g., Case, 1993; Kohlberg, 1981). But because every individual enters the world with a different genetic or biological history, a particular psychological makeup, and idiosyncratic preferences and because individuals develop in varied sociocultural environments (e.g., Ogbu, 1974), their ultimate constructions are unique.

To be sure, the typical *and* unique patterns of human development are complementary, not contradictory or even separate. Our own teaching and research have made this relationship apparent. For instance, we have seen educators make instructional and research decisions seemingly based solely on broad notions of cognitive development, missing strong signs of mental capability evident in the learning environment (e.g., Alexander, Willson, White, & Fuqua, 1987). In contrast, we have witnessed instructional difficulties that emerge when teachers entered the classroom without an understanding of the global developmental patterns that learners of particular ages, experiences, or backgrounds are likely to exhibit (Alexander & Knight, 1993). In essence, optimal learning results when educators understand and appreciate the fluid and complex nature of human change.

But what are the sources of development? Is growth and change in learners the consequence of inheritance or experience? Human growth is influenced by both inherited and experiential factors. It remains debatable as to which of these powerful forces exerts the most influence on learners' growth. Depending on the specific aspects being examined, at times it may appear that changes in human thinking, feeling, or actions are more reflective of one's inherent abilities, capabilities, conditions, or predispositions (e.g., Chomsky, 1986; Scarr, 1992). At other times, the research would seem to support the position that development is more a reflection of one's life experiences and the context in which one learns and grows (e.g., Bronfrenbrenner, 1986; Ogbu, 1974). By strategically acknowledging the potency of both heredity and environment, educators avoid entering this continuing debate.

What It Means

When teachers peer out on the students in their classrooms, they should be able to identify patterns of cognitive, socioemotional, and moral development. Although not all of these patterns are age-specific, teachers should be knowledgeable of the typical developmental levels expected for a particular age or grade. By knowing and understanding these various patterns, teachers can then plan developmentally appropriate activities and tasks that challenge students and enhance learning. But teachers must not be blind to the fact that no two developmental paths are identical. The typical patterns of development are also accented by individual learner differences that can serve to both help and hinder the process of learning.

Rather than ignoring either of these patterns, we would encourage teachers to address both typical patterns and individual differences in their lesson planning. By allowing freedom of choice and agency in developmentally appropriate tasks, teachers will encourage the positive aspects of both typical patterns and individual differences. Finally, teachers should understand that students' heredity and environment contribute to who they are as learners. Although teachers cannot change the students' heredity, they can orchestrate learning environments that match students' general and individualist needs and goals.

Situation or Context

Learning is as much a socially shared undertaking as it is an individually constructed enterprise.

What We Know

The recognition that learning is continuously and markedly shaped by the social context in which it occurs is one of the most powerful observations to emerge in recent psychological literature (e.g., Lave, 1988; Rogoff, 1990). Researchers who investigate the social nature of learning have explored various aspects of this phenomenon, including socially shared cognition (Resnick, Levine, & Teasley, 1991), distributed intelligence (Pea, 1989), shared expertise (Brown & Palincsar, 1989), guided participation (Rogoff, 1990), and anchored instruction (Cognition and Technology Group at Vanderbilt, 1990).

In many ways, the biological structure that separates the individual mind from the sociocultural context in which that mind functions can be thought of as a highly permeable fabric through which thoughts, feelings, and impressions move freely. With each passage through this permeable fabric, these thoughts, feelings, and impressions are filtered and transformed, often without a conscious awareness on the part of the learner or those in the situation or context. Although some filtering may be productive, students may filter out information that does not conform to their preconceived notions (Buehl, Alexander, Murphy, & Sperl, 1999). This is due in part to the fact that schools are, after all, social institutions in which groups of individuals are brought together to share the educational experience. Students are in constant contact with peers and adults during the course of instruction that may encourage them to maintain or change their previous understandings.

One outcome of this growing body of research is the understanding that the context in which learning occurs is certainly nontrivial (Bereiter & Scardamalia, 1989). It is also apparent that the role of the teacher as the facilitator and guide of these social exchanges is vital (Radziszewska & Rogoff, 1988). In essence, when learners were able to benefit from the guidance of a knowledgeable adult (e.g., teacher) who promoted their exploration and interchange, performance was found to be better. It has also been suggested that corresponding with Vygotsky's (1934/1986) concept of a zone of proximal development, the guidance provided by the more knowledgeable and skilled adult or peer should correspond to the knowledge and skills of the learner. Thus as the learner develops in an area or in relation to a given task, then the level of assistance provided by the teacher should decrease proportionately (e.g., Brown & Palincsar, 1989). This lessening of external direction and support from a teacher or adult should theoretically contribute to more independent functioning on the part of the student and likewise enhance the possibility that transfer of the acquired knowledge or skill will occur both in and out of class.

What It Means

Although educators are likely to perceive that the situation or context plays a role in the learning process, they may not understand the depth to which situation or context can help or hinder learning. Indeed, the situation and context influence every aspect of individual and social learning. We would encourage teachers to attend to both individual and social dimensions of learning. In addition, teachers should provide activities (e.g., readings or experiments) that challenge students' views of the world. We are not suggesting that a teacher should reject students' perceptions, but teachers should facilitate student exploration of alternative viewpoints.

One side effect of the socially shared learning movements has been a diminished regard for direct or individual instruction (Alexander & Murphy, 1998). Instead of routinely structuring learning as an independent or collective enterprise, teachers should make grouping decisions thoughtfully and purposefully with consideration of learning goals and student needs. Moreover, even when lessons are focused on group processes, there will likely be times that the teacher will need to intercede and directly teach skills or strategies that will enhance the learning process.

Concluding Remarks

Even though we have explored these five psychological dimensions as separate factors in this discussion, they actually work in concert to promote optimal learning. As researchers, we can theoretically and empirically extract cognition from affect, knowledge from strategic processing, or sociocultural background from development, but these dimensions, along with the others addressed in the principles, remain inextricably intertwined in the real world. For example, the knowledge base is both an aspect of development (e.g., Chi, 1985) and a part of motivation (e.g., Schiefele, 1991). Similarly, development is integrated with individual differences and sociocultural background (e.g., Ogbu, 1974; Scarr, 1992), just as strategic processing is correlated with motivational or affective state (e.g., Hidi & Anderson, 1992).

In light of the interdependence of these dimensions, educators have a greater chance to make significant and long-term changes by approaching learning in a systemic fashion (Salomon, 1991). In his analysis of human behavior and the experiences from which it arises, Dewey (1930) expressed this precept with the words: "No act can be understood apart from the series to which it belongs" (p. 412). We could not agree more. Moreover, as our analysis demonstrates, there is extensive research that upholds the important roles that the knowledge base, strategic processing or executive control, motivation and affect, development and individual differences, and situation or context play in student learning. Embracing and applying the psychological research base encompassed in APA's learner-centered principles can have positive and far-reaching consequences for both teachers and students as the teaching profession progresses into the 21st century.

References and Resources

Alexander, P. A. (1997). Mapping the multidimensional nature of domain learning: The interplay of cognitive, motivational, and strategic forces. In M. L. Maehr & P. R. Pintrich (Eds.), *Advances in motivation and achievement* (Vol. 10, pp. 213-250). Greenwich, CT: JAI.

Alexander, P. A., & Knight, S. L. (1993). Dimensions of the interplay between learning and teaching. *Educational Forum, 57,* 232-245.

Alexander, P. A., Kulikowich, J. M., & Schulze, S. K. (1994). How subject-matter knowledge affects recall and interest on the comprehension of scientific exposition. *American Educational Research Journal, 31,* 313-337.

Alexander, P. A., & Murphy, P. K. (1998). The research base for APA's learner-centered psychological principles. In N. Lambert & B. McCombs (Eds.), *Issues in school reform: A sampler of psychological perspectives on learner-centered schools* (pp. 33-60). Washington, DC: American Psychological Association.

Alexander, P. A., Murphy, P. K., & Woods, B. S. (1996). Of squalls and fathoms: Navigating the seas of educational innovation. *Educational Researcher, 25*(3), 31-36, 39.

Alexander, P. A., Murphy, P. K., & Woods, B. S. (1997). Unearthing academic roots: Educators' perceptions of the interrelationship of philosophy, psychology, and education. *Educational Forum, 61,* 172-186.

Alexander, P. A., Schallert, D. L., & Hare, V. C. (1991). Coming to terms: How researchers in learning and literacy talk about knowledge. *Review of Educational Research, 61,* 315-343.

Alexander, P. A., Willson, V. L., White, C. S., & Fuqua, J. D. (1987). Analogical reasoning in young children. *Journal of Educational Psychology, 79,* 401-408.

American Psychological Association Board of Educational Affairs. (1995, December). *Learner-centered psychological principles: A framework for school redesign and reform* [On-line]. Available: http://www.apa.org/ed/lcp.html

American Psychological Association Presidential Task Force on Psychology in Education. (1993, January). *Learner-centered psychological principles: Guidelines for school redesign and reform.* Washington, DC: American Psychological Association/Midcontinent Regional Educational Laboratory.

Ames, C., & Ames, R. (Eds.). (1989). *Research on motivation in education: The classroom milieu* (Vol. 3). San Diego, CA: Academic Press.

Bandura, A. (1986). *Social foundations of thought and action: A social cognitive theory.* Englewood Cliffs, NJ: Prentice Hall.

Bereiter, C., & Scardamalia, M. (1989). Intentional learning as a goal of instruction. In L. B. Resnick (Ed.), *Knowing, learning, and instruction: Essays in honor of Robert Glaser* (pp. 361-392). Hillsdale, NJ: Lawrence Erlbaum.

Borkowski, J. G., Carr, M., & Pressley, M. (1987). "Spontaneous" strategy use: Perspectives from metacognitive theory. *Intelligence, 11,* 61-75.

Bronfrenbrenner, U. (1986). Ecology of the family as a context for human development: Research perspectives. *Developmental Psychology, 22,* 723-742.

Brown, A. L., & Palincsar, A. S. (1989). Guided, cooperative learning and individual knowledge acquisition. In L. B. Resnick (Ed.), *Knowing, learning, and instruction: Essays in honor of Robert Glaser* (pp. 393-451). Hillsdale, NJ: Lawrence Erlbaum.

Buehl, M. M., Alexander, P. A., Murphy, P. K., & Sperl, C. T. (in press). Profiling persuasion: The role of beliefs, knowledge, and interest in the processing of persuasive texts that vary by argument structure. *Journal of Literacy Research.*

Case, R. (1993). Theories of learning and theories of development. *Educational Psychologist, 28,* 219-233.

Chambliss, M. J., & Garner, R. (1996). Do adults change their minds after reading persuasive text? *Written Communication, 13*(3), 291-313.

Chi, M. T. H. (1985). Interactive roles of knowledge and strategies in the development of organized sorting and recall. In S. F. Chipman, J. W. Segal, & R. Glaser (Eds.), *Thinking and learning skills: Research and open questions* (Vol. 2, pp. 457-483). Hillsdale, NJ: Lawrence Erlbaum.

Chinn, C. A., & Brewer, W. F. (1993). The role of anomalous data in knowledge acquisition: A theoretical framework and implications for science instruction. *Review of Educational Research, 63,* 1-49.

Chomsky, N. (1986). *Knowledge of language: Its nature, origin, and use.* New York: Praeger.

Cognition and Technology Group at Vanderbilt. (1990). Anchored instruction and its relationship to situated cognition. *Educational Researcher, 19*(6), 2-10.

Dewey, J. (1930). Conduct and experience. In C. Murchism (Ed.), *Psychologies of 1930* (pp. 410-429). Worchester, MA: Clark University Press.

Gardner, H. (1993). *Creating minds.* New York: Basic Books.

Garner, R. (1990). When children and adults do not use learning strategies: Toward a theory of settings. *Review of Educational Research, 60,* 517-529.

Garner, R., & Alexander, P. A. (1989). Metacognition: Answered and unanswered questions. *Educational Psychologist, 24,* 143-148.

Hidi, S., & Anderson, V. (1992). Situational interest and its impact on reading and expository writing. In K. A. Renninger, S. Hidi, & A. Krapp (Eds.), *The role of interest in learning and development* (pp. 215-238). Hillsdale, NJ: Lawrence Erlbaum.

Kohlberg, L. (1981). *The philosophy of moral development.* New York: Harper & Row.

Lambert, N. M., & McCombs, B. L. (Eds.). (1998). *How students learn: Reforming schools through learner-centered education.* Washington, DC: American Psychological Association.

Lave, J. (1988). *Cognition in practice.* Cambridge, UK: Cambridge University Press.

Lipson, M. Y. (1983). The influence of religious affiliation on children's memory for text information. *Reading Research Quarterly, 18,* 448-457.

McCombs, B. L. (1998). Integrating metacognition, affect, and motivation in improving teacher education. In N. Lambert & B. L. McCombs (Eds.), *Issues in school reform: A sampler of psychological perspectives on learner-centered schools* (pp. 379-408). Washington, DC: American Psychological Association.

McCombs, B. L., & Whisler, P. T. (1997). *The learner centered classroom and school: Strategies for enhancing student motivation and achievement.* San Francisco: Jossey-Bass.

Murphy, P. K., & Alexander, P. A. (2000). A motivated exploration of motivation terminology. *Contemporary Educational Psychology, 25,* 3-53.

National Commission on Excellence in Education. (1983). *A nation at risk.* Washington, DC: U.S. Department of Education.

Ogbu, J. U. (1974). *The next generation: An ethnography of education in an urban neighborhood.* New York: Academic Press.

Palincsar, A. S., & Brown, A. L. (1984). Reciprocal teaching of comprehension-fostering and monitoring activities. *Cognition and Instruction, 1,* 117-175.

Pea, R. D. (1989). Socializing the knowledge transfer problem. *International Journal of Educational Research, 2,* 639-663.

Radziszewska, B., & Rogoff, B. (1988). Influence of adult and peer collaboration on children's planning skills. *Developmental Psychology, 24,* 840-848.

Resnick, L. B. (1991). Shared cognition. In L. B. Resnick, J. M. Levine, & S. D. Teasley (Eds.), *Perspectives on socially shared cognition* (pp. 1-20). Washington, DC: American Psychological Association.

Resnick, L. B., Levine, J. M., & Teasley, S. D. (1991). *Perspectives on socially shared cognition.* Washington, DC: American Psychological Association.

Reynolds, R. E., & Shirey, L. L. (1988). The role of attention in studying and learning. In C. E. Weinstein, E. T. Goetz, & P. A. Alexander (Eds.), *Learning and study strategies: Issues in assessment, instruction, and evaluation* (pp. 77-100). San Diego, CA: Academic Press.

Rogoff, B. (1990). *Apprenticeship in thinking: Cognitive development in social context.* New York: Oxford University Press.

Salomon, G. (1991). Transcending the qualitative-quantitative debate: The analytic and systemic approach to educational research. *Educational Psychologist, 20*(6), 10-18.

Scarr, S. (1992). Developmental theories for the 1990's: Development and individual differences. *Child Development, 63,* 1-19.

Schiefele, U. (1991). Interest, learning, and motivation. *Educational Psychologist, 26,* 229-323.

Vygotsky, L. (1986). *Thought and language* (A. Kozulin, Trans.). Cambridge: MIT Press. (Original work published 1934)

CHAPTER 3

Achieving High-Level Outcomes for All Students

The Meaning of Staff-Shared Understanding and Commitment

Fred M. Newmann
University of Wisconsin–Madison

Summary

- Schools enhance student performance and minimize disparities in student achievement when their teachers demonstrate shared understanding of and commitment to high-level outcomes for all students.

- High-level outcomes require attention to three criteria for intellectual quality: selection of significant curriculum content, accuracy and precision, and teaching for in-depth understanding.

- Staff in effective schools use a common language directed toward a specific intellectual mission, rather than vague slogans such as "All students can learn." There is continuous debate and inquiry about how best to achieve the school's intellectual mission. For example,

AUTHOR'S NOTE: The initial draft of this chapter was prepared at the Center on Organization and Restructuring of Schools, supported by the U.S. Department of Education, Office of Educational Research and Improvement (Grant No. R117Q00005-95) and by the Wisconsin Center for Education Research, School of Education, University of Wisconsin–Madison. The opinions expressed in this publication are those of the author and do not necessarily reflect the views of the supporting agencies.

before adopting proposed new techniques of teaching, assessment, and student management or new programs for student support, teachers inquire critically about the potential of new practices to elevate the intellectual quality of student work.

- Teachers' shared understanding of high-level outcomes is supported by collective commitment to the work for the achievement of all the school's students, not just the students they teach. This involves professional norms of high expectations, respect, and caring among students and staff.

- To establish high expectations for all students, effective schools use common standards and curriculum, as well as approaches to teaching that allow for differential responses to students' unique backgrounds and interests.

- The school culture reflected in the above points requires strong instructional leadership by the principal and is often facilitated by structures for teaming, teaching, and professional development that allow students and teachers to know one another well. Schools maximize the likelihood of achieving high-level outcomes for all students when the staff shares an understanding of and commitment to outcomes of high intellectual quality. The following synthesis of research is intended to clarify the meaning and importance of these ideas.[1]

High-Level Outcomes

In schools striving for high-level outcomes, teachers give primary attention to the intellectual quality of student work. In defining high-level outcomes, or student work of high intellectual quality, teachers pay close attention to three criteria: teaching significant curriculum content; accuracy and precision in teaching and student performance; and in-depth understanding in teaching and student performance.

Significant Curriculum Content. The effort to develop standards for curriculum and assessment in the United States illustrates major difficulties in arriving at national consensus on the most significant content to teach all students. Because of the modern knowledge explosion, it is impossible to teach everything worth knowing; some knowledge must be selected as more important to teach and other knowledge omitted from the curriculum. Because of conflicting social perspectives on knowledge and education, selecting the most significant knowledge to teach is highly controversial, and pressure continues to teach massive amounts of information and skills.

Effective schools, nevertheless, devote serious effort to deciding what knowledge and skills are most important, most authoritative and up-to-date in legitimate fields of knowledge, and most likely to be useful to their students in further education and life. Teachers in these schools do not teach material simply because it appears in a text or is required on a test. They think about and consciously decide which content and skills are substantively worthwhile and backed by the authority of respectable research. To help with these decisions, teachers have used outlines of significant, challenging curriculum developed by national professional organizations and curriculum projects of districts and states. But regardless of the specific sources of content, teachers in effective schools make a special effort to avoid giving students a trivial curriculum or busywork. Instead, they try to ensure that the curriculum offers legitimate intellectual substance at all grades to all students.

Accuracy and Precision. In effective schools, when teachers help students learn facts, concepts, theories, algorithms, and conventions for written and oral communication, they emphasize and celebrate "getting it right." Assignments may call for more than one "right answer," but even when the solution is ambiguous or when more than one response can be considered well grounded, teachers insist that students' statements be consistent with authoritative knowledge in the relevant discipline or area of expertise. Communicating clearly and precisely is also important. Teachers help students pay scrupulous attention to style and detail so that students will learn to avoid misrepresentation and say exactly what they mean so that it is properly understood. This concern for accuracy and precision extends to teachers' evaluation of the materials they use, to the discussions they hold with one another, and to their own teaching behavior.

In-Depth Understanding. Significant curriculum content and accuracy and precision in representing it are important to high-level intellectual work, but they are not sufficient. In addition, students must show they can think critically and creatively. They must go beyond recitation of isolated facts and definitions, beyond superficial awareness of a large body of information and proper use of basic skills, to organizing, synthesizing, and interpreting this knowledge. High-level intellectual performance illustrates construction of knowledge aimed at in-depth understanding of what is studied. To achieve in-depth understanding, teachers in effective schools limit the scope of the curriculum so they can spend more time exploring the complexities and nuances of fewer topics. And they help students to see how real-life issues that challenge the intellect can be illuminated and often resolved through application of academic learning.

Effective schools that aim primarily toward conventional measures of student achievement may put less emphasis on in-depth understanding, with greater attention to accuracy and precision in learning significant content. Effective schools that pursue more authentic intellectual work put high priority on in-depth understanding.

Ideally, most teachers might agree with these criteria for intellectual quality. But in practice, teachers in schools differ enormously in the intellectual resources they offer and in the intellectual rigor they expect from students. Apart from teacher differences within schools, some whole schools succeed far more than others in emphasizing high-level intellectual outcomes.

Shared Understanding and Commitment

In effective schools, teachers exercise individual discretion over their teaching and use unique classroom styles, but their professional individuality is guided by and subjected to shared understandings of and collective schoolwide commitments to high intellectual outcomes.

As teachers talk with one another and with students about the kind of achievement they expect, they use a common language that communicates a specific intellectual mission for the school. One example is a school that emphasized five "habits of mind," such as identifying the perspective of an author and assessing the quality of evidence presented; another school, which emphasized complex thinking and problem solving connected to real-world issues, summarized its mission as "applied learning." Some schools focus on a list of competencies that all students are expected to master to graduate to the next level of schooling. Other schools establish a common agenda for learning by requiring all students to take a specific set of classes, each being taught according to criteria for intellectual quality such as those discussed above.

Some schools forge mission statements that may represent shared understanding and consensus but concentrate more on the logistics of techniques and procedures than on the intellectual quality of student work. Cooperative learning, hands-on activities, advanced technology, portfolio assessment, and community-based learning are examples of procedures or techniques that alone reflect no particular intellectual goals. In effective schools, however, the intellectual goals remain so paramount that before adopting proposed new programs or practices, the staff scrutinize them to make sure they are likely to promote high-level intellectual outcomes.

Teachers in effective schools have common understandings of their main intellectual goals, but unanimity on intellectual mission does not entail mechanical, uniform compliance with a "party line"; routinized teaching; or a static, rigid curriculum. To the contrary, shared understanding of and collective commitment to central goals often stimulates lively faculty debate on how best to achieve the goals. Staff discussion often entails a continuous loop of asking how to improve; trying new approaches; evaluating them; and redesigning the curriculum, assessment, and teaching. This process provokes reconsideration of the goals themselves. But discussion over priorities and possible changes is conducted in ways that reinforce shared understanding and schoolwide consensus.

In effective schools, student success with high-level outcomes becomes a collective responsibility of the staff. That is, teachers work to enhance not only their own students' learning but that of other students as well, for example, by helping to enforce standards of intellect and conduct throughout the school, even when it may involve possible conflict with colleagues. This norm—that all teachers are responsible for all students—helps to sustain each teacher's commitment. It puts peer pressure to be more accountable on those staff who may not have carried their fair share. And collective responsibility offers support to those teachers who may previously have worked alone and beyond the call of duty, yet still felt unable to help some students.

Teachers demonstrate commitment to high standards by working long hours to improve their practice and to support students. Teachers in effective schools have confidence in their students' potential even when the students' lives beyond school present enormous challenges to physical, social, and emotional development. When students face conditions that deprive them of opportunities to engage in concentrated study and undermine their will to achieve, these teachers do not give up on students. They insist that it is the teachers' and students' responsibility to beat the odds and to overcome possible failures of the past in school and beyond.

To hold all students to high intellectual standards, teachers offer special help and support, not only through individualized teaching and tutoring but also by establishing important norms of confidence, respect, and caring. These teachers convey confidence that students will earn success through hard work on academic tasks; they reinforce student peers for careful listening, responding seriously to one another's concerns, and helping one another with schoolwork; they provide a "safe" environment where students have the opportunity to make mistakes and to try again without being judged "stupid."

Helping Diverse Students Achieve: Commonality and Differentiation

Perhaps the greatest challenge that teachers confront daily is how to cope with diversity among students. Students come to class with different levels of competence and academic preparation, different degrees of motivation to succeed in schoolwork, different cultural backgrounds, different intellectual interests, different social skills and levels of maturity. The persisting dilemma is how to respect and address individual differences and at the same time maximize the success of all with high-level intellectual work. In effective schools, teachers walk a tightrope between two prominent approaches in the handling of student diversity.

One approach insists that in spite of student diversity, all students must study a common curriculum and be required to meet the same specific high standards for success. Advocates of "common" student experiences point to dangers of catering excessively to student differences through special programs and curriculum tracking that have persistently delivered lower-quality education to students of lower socioeconomic status, students of color, and students with histories of school failure. Since highly differentiated programs have led to blatant educational inequities, advocates of common experiences prefer to compel all students to enroll in a common, high-quality program. The common approach may minimize the inequities of excessive differentiation, but it also poses a danger. Curriculum, teaching, and assessment offered only in a single, standard form can make it difficult for students from unique backgrounds to master the material and to succeed; if there is no flexibility to respond to students' unique needs, these students may lose interest, fail, and drop out.

The second approach is to take students' diverse backgrounds more prominently into account and design special curricula, classes, and programs to address these directly. The intent is not to relax intellectual standards but to use different avenues to development of the intellect rather than expecting all students to conform to a single, common path. Some students may be assigned to remedial programs to boost basic competencies enough so that they can eventually participate in a mainstream college prep curriculum. Or students may enroll in different career cluster programs to help them channel their efforts toward economically productive pursuits that may not require 4 years of college. The differentiation of student programs avoids trying to fit all students into one mold, but it too involves a big risk: Some programs tend to perpetuate much lower intellectual standards than others.

Effective schools usually use both commonality and differentiation in curriculum, teaching, and assessment, but in doing so they exploit the advantages and guard against the abuses of each. For example, when the same curriculum and assessments are required of all students, special efforts are made to help students who may be ill prepared, perhaps through additional remedial and tutorial work, and tailoring daily assignments to students' different topical interests. In contrast, when students are grouped in different programs, such as English as a second language or bilingual, gifted and talented, college prep, or vocational, special efforts are made to ensure that the highest expectations for intellectual work permeate every class.

Theoretically, both commonality and differentiation have the potential to boost students to high levels of achievement. But since each harbors the possibility of major disservice to less educationally advanced students, the key is to fashion a creative combination. Research has not identified a specific mix of common and differentiated experiences that works for the teaching of all subjects to all students. But regardless of how these programmatic issues are resolved, more effective schools reflect schoolwide consensus on reasonably specific intellectual standards that all students are expected to master.

Making It Happen

Research describes what it means for schools to have shared understanding of and commitment to high-level outcomes for all students and documents the effectiveness of such schools. How to change schools to increase shared understanding of and commitment to high-level outcomes is another story. Research is less conclusive on this issue but does offer important insights about specific difficulties that need to be addressed and some findings on steps that might be taken.

Difficulties

It may seem self-evident that schools should focus centrally on the intellectual goals of education, but for many schools this is remarkably difficult. Why? First, teachers, parents, and students are also seriously occupied with other tasks and goals for schooling. To develop students' intellect, schools must provide a safe and orderly environment and they must socialize students to behave as responsible members of the school. In addition, schools are expected to instill democratic values, to contribute to students' physical and emotional health, to offer engaging extracurricular activities, to provide adult supervision when parents are not available, and to facilitate student placement in jobs and further schooling. Teachers and administrators spend a good deal of time trying to maintain an orderly environment conducive to learning and trying to achieve the other legitimate goals of school. Sometimes preoccupation with these activities deflects attention from the quality of student learning. As staff became involved with issues of student conduct, with supervision of extracurricular activities, with administrative and managerial tasks such as taking attendance or keeping records, and with students' and parents' emotional concerns, intellectual priorities slip into the background.

Second, reform initiatives themselves generate a host of new issues that can divert staff attention from the intellectual agenda for learning. For example, adoption of techniques such as cooperative learning groups, use of portfolios, or student independent research projects raise issues of how to manage and supervise students. Adoption of shared governance and team planning expands the potential for interpersonal conflict and power struggles. When significant reforms are implemented without full faculty support, sometimes reformers understandably become more preoccupied with how to generate support within the school than with the intellectual quality of teacher and student work.

Third, striving for high intellectual quality is demanding work for both teachers and students. In typical schools, when goals are vague or when consensus about basic school purpose is low, it becomes easy for both teachers and students to avoid high standards for performance. Or when more specific high standards are advocated, but teachers and students perceive significant risk of failure, it becomes easy to cite students' special circumstances or differences in prior preparation to justify less rigorous instruction, curriculum, and assessment.

In effective schools, in spite of other goals for education and a tendency in the profession at large to focus more on programs and techniques than intellectual quality, the intellectual focus of education remains central, but not to the neglect of students' social and emotional needs. Effective schools offer caring and personally supportive environments for students, but this support is clearly connected to pursuit of high-level intellectual outcomes. And although pursuing high-level outcomes for all students is exceptionally hard work, teachers in effective schools get the support to do it.

First Steps and Key Supports

To deliberately build a school mission focused on high-level intellectual outcomes, the staff must understand the distinction between techniques, activities, and processes of schooling and the kind of cognitive work and intellectual accomplishments to be valued and promoted. The staff must craft a language to identify intellectual outcomes that teachers from all the grade levels and subject areas in the school can endorse. This language needs to be general enough to communicate useful goals for different grade levels and subjects, but specific enough to be recognized as high-level intellectual work. Those in particular grade levels and subject areas can then add more specificity to the general standards by detailing the substantive content to be taught.

Success in these first steps requires strong leadership from the school administration. Administrators must show their commitment by allocating resources and arranging structural conditions that also support other themes in this book, such as open communication and collaborative problem solving, ongoing assessment of teaching and learning, and continuous professional development.

For example, nurturing and sustaining the high expectations and culture of respect among students along with the trusting, collaborative professional culture among staff characteristic of effective schools depends on teachers and students being able to know one another well. Effective schools promote these norms not only by hiring personnel committed to this view of schooling but also by crafting structures for teacher teaming, teaching, and professional development that permit teachers and students to spend significant amounts of time together. Many effective schools arrange for one or more of the following: Teachers instruct the same group of students for several hours a day or for 2 or more years; teachers in a grade level have several hours per week of common planning time; teachers have time to observe one another teaching and to confer about their observations; the entire staff spends several days a year in staff development sessions working on a common schoolwide issue. These structural supports, combined with administrative leadership, selective hiring, and strategic allocation of technical resources, all aimed toward shared understanding of high-level outcomes, should maximize the opportunity for staff to respond well to student differences while maintaining commitment to high expectations for all.

Answers to Likely Questions From Teachers

Question 1. Often there seems to be a conflict between teaching the multitude of basic facts and skills required by standardized tests and teaching to higher-level outcomes. How do teachers in the most effective schools handle this problem?

Answer. There is no conclusive research on how teachers handle the problem. But there is evidence that teaching to higher-level outcomes does not jeopardize student scores on standardized tests. In fact, studies indicate that teaching to higher-level outcomes tends to boost student scores on standardized tests.[2] The most effective teachers probably do not try to "cover everything," but decide what aspects of a subject or skill are really most important. They teach these topics in depth to promote high levels of understanding and competence. Deep knowledge and high mastery in the essential areas then transfer to assisting students in figuring out answers to many questions or problems that have not been explicitly studied.

Question 2. Common high-level outcomes and a common curriculum for all students is a fine ideal, but aren't there situations when it helps to group students according to their achievement levels or interests and to vary instruction and assessment between groups?

Answer. Yes. For example, effective elementary school reading programs group students in achievement levels and design instruction accordingly. But the dangers of permanent tracking are avoided by staff holding high expectations that all students reach a common level of reading proficiency by a certain point (e.g., Grade 3) and by periodic assessment and regrouping based on reading performance (e.g., every 9 weeks). At the high school level, although some students are enrolled in college prep programs and others in vocational or technical programs, many schools have aimed for common high standards of academic achievement by enriching the curriculum of the vocational or technical programs.[3]

Question 3. In some schools, a significant number of teachers may be burned out, just coasting toward retirement, or for other reasons not interested in collaborating to build shared understanding of and commitment to high-level outcomes. How can schools develop a shared mission when many teachers don't want to cooperate?

Answer. Different strategies are needed, depending on whether teachers seem to be resisting because of reasonable or unreasonable concerns. Reasonable concerns could include any of the following: (a) "Since we have tried many reforms in the past that were either abandoned very quickly or showed no signs of success, why should I have any confidence that this reform effort will succeed?" (b) "Collaboration to reach some common standards sounds like a good idea, but this will take lots of time and effort, and I'm already working 50 hours a week." (c) "The prospect of collaborating is scary, because I'm not sure how to handle criticism of my teaching and not sure I can give helpful feedback to others." These concerns need to be addressed by showing faculty the research on effective schools; by offering sufficient administrative support to give teachers time to develop their mission; and by providing opportunities for productive sharing in an intellectually honest, but personally supportive and trusting, environment.

Teachers who resist because of unreasonable concerns include those who believe so strongly that educationally disadvantaged students will never succeed in school that they refuse to discuss the issue; those who insist that they must be left alone in their classrooms as professionals to do whatever they think best; and those who don't care whether their students succeed or fail, but just show up on the job to collect a paycheck. If such teachers exist in a school and interfere with efforts of others to build a school mission aimed at high-level outcomes, the administration must move them out of the school or isolate them sufficiently to minimize their negative effect on the collective effort.

Question 4. Don't you need support for high-level outcomes from students' homes, and what should teachers do if that support just isn't there for many students?

Answer. Research has shown effective ways for schools to reach out to gain parents' trust, support, and participation. The specific strategies are too numerous to mention here.[4] But when parents feel comfortable talking with teachers, when teachers explain what it means to teach toward high-level outcomes and why this is important for their children's success, and when parents see their children actually producing higher-quality work, most parents are likely to give enthusiastic support for it at home.

Notes

1. This chapter is a synthesis of sources of evidence and analysis of school effectiveness listed in the References and Resources. A useful definition for an "effective" school is one with a record of high student achievement on either conventional tests or more authentic assessments, in which disparities in achievement between students of different socioeconomic, racial/ethnic, and gender groups are minimal.

2. These studies include research on the teaching of mathematics, reading, and writing to disadvantaged students (Knapp, Shields, & Turnbull, 1992; Lee, Smith, & Newmann, in press); teaching mathematics in Grades 1, 2, and 8 (Carpenter, Fennema, Peterson, Chiang, & Loef, 1989; Cobb et al., 1991; Silver & Lane, 1995); teaching reading in Grades 1, 2, and 3 (Tharp, 1982); teaching mathematics and science in high school (Lee, Smith, & Croninger, 1997); and teaching social studies in high school (Levin, Newmann, & Oliver, 1969).

3. Success for All is an example of the approach to achievement grouping in reading (www.successforall.net); High Schools That Work is a program that works toward common high-level outcomes for both college prep and vocational programs (www.sreb.org).

4. For more information and assistance in developing comprehensive programs of school, family, and community partnerships that support school goals for student success, contact the National Network of Partnership Schools at Johns Hopkins by visiting the Web site: www.partnershipschools.org. Also see Epstein, Coates, Salinas, Sanders, and Simon (1997); Lueder (1998); and National PTA (2000).

References and Resources

Each reference is coded to indicate which one of five general issues in this chapter it addresses most directly. A reference may address more than one issue, but only the most prominent is indicated.

1 = Review or synthesis of research on school effectiveness

2 = Empirical study of the meaning and importance of shared understanding and commitment to high-level outcomes

3 = Study of the issue of commonality and differentiation in instruction

4 = Study of organizational conditions that promote shared understanding and commitment to high-level outcomes

5 = Study of the effects of teaching for high-level outcomes on conventional achievement test scores

---

1 Bliss, J. R., Firestone, W. A., & Richards, C. E. (1991). *Rethinking effective schools: Research and practice*. Englewood Cliffs, NJ: Prentice Hall.

2 Bryk, A. S., & Driscoll, M. E. (1988). *The high school as community: Contextual influences, and consequences for students and teachers*. Madison: University of Wisconsin–Madison, National Center on Effective Secondary Schools.

2 Bryk, A. S., Lee, V. E., & Holland, P. B. (1993). *Catholic schools and the common good*. Cambridge, MA: Harvard University Press.

5 Carpenter, T. P., Fennema, E., Peterson, P. L., Chiang, C., & Loef, M. (1989). Using knowledge of children's mathematics thinking in classroom teaching: An experimental study. *American Educational Research Journal, 26*(4), 499-531.

5 Cobb, P., Wood, T., Yackel, E., Nicholls, J., Wheatley, G., Trigatti, B., & Perlwitz, M. (1991). Assessment of a problem-centered second-grade mathematics project. *Journal for Research in Mathematics Education, 22*(1), 2-29.

2 Coleman, J. S., & Hoffer, T. (1987). *Public and private high schools: The impact of communities*. New York: Basic Books.

2 Edmonds, R. R., & Frederiksen, J. R. (1979). *The search for effective schools: The identification and analysis of city schools that are instructionally effective for poor children*. Washington, DC. (ERIC Document Reproduction Service No. ED170396)

4 Epstein, J. L., Coates, L., Salinas, K. C., Sanders, M. G., & Simon, B. S. (1997). *School, family, and community partnerships: Your handbook for action*. Thousand Oaks, CA: Corwin.

5 Knapp, M. S., Shields, P. M., & Turnbull, B. J. (1992). *Academic challenge for the children of poverty: Summary report*. Washington, DC: Office of Policy and Planning, U.S. Department of Education.

1 Kyle, R. M. J., & White, E. H. (Eds.). (1985). *Reaching for excellence: An effective schools sourcebook*. Washington, DC: National Institute of Education.

1 Lee, V. E., Bryk, A., & Smith, J. B. (1993). The organization of effective secondary schools. *Review of Research in Education, 19*, 171-267.

4 Lee, V. E., & Smith, J. B. (1995). Effects of high school restructuring and size on gains in achievement and engagement for early secondary school students. *Sociology of Education, 68*(4), 241-270.

5 Lee, V. E., Smith, J. B., & Croninger, R. G. (1997). How high school organization influences the equitable distribution of learning in mathematics and science. *Sociology of Education, 70,* 128-150.

5 Lee, V. E., Smith, J. B., & Newmann, F. M. (in press). *Instruction and achievement in Chicago elementary schools.* Chicago: Consortium on Chicago School Research.

5 Levin, M., Newmann, F. M., & Oliver, D. W. (1969). *A law and social studies curriculum based on the analysis of public issues: A final report.* Washington, DC: Office of Education, Bureau of Research, U.S. Department of Health, Education, and Welfare.

4 Little, J. W. (1982). Norms of collegiality and experimentation: Workplace conditions of school success. *American Educational Research Journal, 19*(3), 325-340.

4 Little, J. W., & McLaughlin, M. W. (Eds.). (1993). *Teachers' work: Individuals, colleagues, and contexts.* New York: Teachers College Press.

2 Louis, K. S., Kruse, S. D., & Marks, H. M. (1996). School wide professional community. In F. M. Newmann & Associates (Eds.), *Authentic achievement: Restructuring schools for intellectual quality* (pp. 179-203). San Francisco: Jossey-Bass.

4 Lueder, D. (1998). *Creating partnerships with parents.* Lancaster, PA: Technomic.

4 Marks, H. M., Doane, K. B., & Secada, W. G. (1996). Support for student achievement. In F. M. Newmann & Associates (Eds.), *Authentic achievement: Restructuring schools for intellectual quality* (pp. 209-227). San Francisco: Jossey-Bass.

4 National PTA. (2000). *Building successful partnerships.* Bloomington, IN: National Educational Service.

4 Newmann, F. M., & Associates. (1996). *Authentic achievement: Restructuring schools for intellectual quality.* San Francisco: Jossey-Bass.

4 Newmann, F. M., Smith, B., & Allensworth, E. (in press). *School reform with focus: Benefits and challenges of instructional program coherence.* Chicago: Consortium on Chicago School Research.

4 Newmann, F. M., & Wehlage, G. G. (1995). *Successful school restructuring: A report to the public and educators.* Madison: Center on Organization and Restructuring of Schools, Wisconsin Center for Education Research, University of Wisconsin.

3 Oakes, J., Gamoran, A., & Page, R. N. (1992). Curriculum differentiation: Opportunities, outcomes, and meanings. In P. W. Jackson (Ed.), *Handbook of research on curriculum: A project of the American Educational Research Association* (pp. 570-608). New York: Macmillan.

4 Popkewitz, T. S., Tabachnik, B. R., & Wehlage, G. G. (1982). *The myth of educational reform: A study of school responses to a program of change.* Madison: University of Wisconsin Press.

1 Purkey, S. C., & Smith, M. S. (1983). Effective schools: A review. *Elementary School Journal, 83*(4), 427-452.

2 Rutter, M., Maughan, B., Mortimore, P., & Ouston, J. (1979). *Fifteen thousand hours: Secondary schools and their effects on children.* Cambridge, MA: Harvard University Press.

3 Secada, W. G., Gamoran, D., & Weinstein, M. G. (1996). Pathways to equity. In F. M. Newmann & Associates (Eds.), *Authentic achievement: Restructuring schools for intellectual quality* (pp. 228-244). San Francisco: Jossey-Bass.

5 Silver, E., & Lane, S. (1995). Can instructional reform in urban middle schools help students narrow the mathematics performance gap? *Research in Middle Level Education, 18*(2), 49-70.

3 Slavin, R. E. (1987). Ability grouping and achievement in elementary schools: A best-evidence synthesis. *Review of Educational Research, 57*(3), 293-336.

3 Slavin, R. E. (1990). Achievement effects of ability grouping in secondary schools: A best-evidence synthesis. *Review of Educational Research, 60*(3), 471-499.

5 Tharp, R. G. (1982). The effects instruction of comprehension: Results and description of the Kamehameha Early Education Program. *Reading Research Quarterly, 17*(4), 503-527.

Professional Communication and Collaboration

Judith Warren Little
University of California, Berkeley

C entral to the vigor and success of a school is the strength of its teacher workforce. This discussion focuses on one source of strength—the fabric of teachers' professional relationships. Drawing from the past two decades of research on teachers' work and experience in school improvement, my aim is to supply schools with a way of thinking about the school's role in contributing to the professional relationships experienced by teachers. I have concentrated my attention on teachers, but the same arguments could reasonably be made for administrators, counselors, paraprofessionals, and other specialists.

Strong and Weak Ties Among Teachers— What Does the School Promote?

Consider what kind of "communication maps" might be generated by shadowing several individual teachers for a week. The likely scenarios vary widely. At one extreme, we would expect to find teachers who spend entire days without more than a few words to another teacher and whose professional interactions are sporadic at best. Such teachers embody the enduring image of the isolated teacher behind the closed classroom door—nodes in the communication net are few and widely spaced, having minimal significance for the teacher's life and work. At the other extreme, we would

43

find teachers whose week is crowded with professional encounters both inside and outside the school. In this scenario, the classroom walls are more permeable and the communication net is more densely and color-fully woven; teachers see themselves as members of one or more professional communities that may range from small, intimate partnerships to far-flung networks. Between these extremes, the possibilities multiply.

The variety in these communication maps derives in part from the qualities or circumstances of individual teachers. Aspects of personality, attitudes toward teaching, teaching workload, and family obligations all may shape teachers' disposition to forge close ties with their colleagues. Despite these individual differences, it nonetheless remains evident that the school itself influences the nature and extent of teachers' professional communication and collaboration. Schools have been shown to vary in the professional cultures they support and thus in the typical configuration of communication one finds among teachers. It follows that schools might more deliberately promote and organize the kinds of professional exchange that benefit teaching and learning.

Research and experience enable schools to assess the kinds of professional communication that they foster and the ways in which that communication influences teacher knowledge, belief, practice, and commitment. Is a given school an "isolating" place to work, a place that breeds cliques and factions, a place that fosters innovation by creative individualists, an environment that cultivates close collaboration? All in all, what kinds of professional contacts and ties are valued and supported, and which are disparaged or deemed unimportant?[1]

Schools That Isolate

On the whole, both the traditions of teaching and the architecture of the school reinforce privacy and independence, making truly vigorous colleagueship both rare and relatively unstable. An isolating school does little to cultivate new traditions or to mediate the "cellular" structure of separate classrooms joined mainly by a common parking lot. Indeed, it may intensify isolation by the way it organizes time, space, responsibilities, or resources and by permitting a culture of protective individualism community.

The communication maps characteristic of isolating schools show that exchanges would be infrequent, short, and dominated by personal (non-teaching) topics. Beginning teachers would struggle on their own, reporting no offers of help. Teachers would profess little knowledge of one another's teaching and little familiarity with students outside their own classes. Time available outside the classroom would be limited and would be devoted to individual pursuits-planning, grading papers, calling parents, taking a break—but not to collaborative work related to teaching. Teachers would find it difficult to secure resources for out-of-school professional activities (conferences, school visits, etc.). The overall atmosphere might range from congenial to toxic, but in any event would engage teachers rarely on matters of teaching.

Schools That Support the "Independent Artisan"

Many teachers, considering their own circumstances, would find the portrait of extreme isolation to be overdrawn. Although working primarily on their own classroom pursuits, they would deny being isolated from the company of colleagues or from new ideas, methods, or materials. Their portrait would coincide well with what Michael Huberman (1993) has termed the "independent artisan." Huberman maintains, "The vision of the schoolhouse as a bonded community of adults and children is . . . an unlikely vision to transport into real life" (p. 11). The image of the independent artisan conducting small experiments within the privacy of the classroom, he argues, is more readily consistent with the nature of teachers' work: the structural separation of the classroom, the immediate and specific demands of classroom life, the egalitarian traditions of teaching. This model receives additional support from other researchers who have shown that teachers may have good and pressing reasons to preserve their independence.

In a school that fosters independent artisanry, the communication maps would show teachers pursuing periodic contacts with colleagues (often outside the school) that expand their resources for the classroom. Teachers would respond readily to requests for help, share materials on occasion, and have access to resources for professional development. However, the communication maps would be unlikely to show instances of deep and sustained collaboration or evidence that teachers were closely familiar with one another's teaching practices.

At its best, the independent artisan model might result in a school that takes pride in being a collection of highly individual, but capable, innovating teachers and in supplying teachers with incentives and resources for the innovations they undertake. Missing from the model, however, is any provision for moving collectively on schoolwide priorities or any mechanism for ensuring that all that independent "tinkering" serves students well.

Schools With Collaborative Cultures

Research of the past two decades confirms the power of professional community to heighten teachers' efficacy and strengthen the overall capacity of a school to engage in change. Increasingly, we also find evidence that some conditions, especially a collective responsibility for student success, are clearly associated with student achievement. Yet the same research illustrates the complexities of teacher community, distinguishing the various dimensions and contexts of collegiality. The work that teachers undertake together may be ambitious or superficial; the relationships they establish may be harmonious or conflict ridden. Recent investigations have uncovered prospects for balkanization, the underestimated potential for conflict among teachers working closely together, the difficult balance between collaborative endeavors and individual interests, and the sheer demand that collaboration places on time and energy.

Not all forms of professional solidarity are good for schools. Teachers may be deeply divided in their beliefs about teaching, learning, or other matters, giving rise to contentious and enduring micropolitical battles (Ball, 1987). Groups may derive their "strength" from like-mindedness that has little to do with educational good—shared cynicism or elitism, for example. They may be provided time and resources to collaborate, but for a purpose they neither developed nor value—a problem Hargreaves (1991) labels "contrived collegiality."

Genuine teacher learning communities—those with a demonstrable effect on teaching and learning—have a distinctive character. They question—and challenge—teaching practices when they prove ineffective with students and routinely investigate new conceptions of teaching and learning. They respect the creative contributions and passions of individuals, but are able to ask one another tough questions. Such groups maintain an open curiosity about their own practices and tolerate informed dissent. As McLaughlin and Talbert (in press) observe, "teacher learning community is not simply the collection of good and committed teachers." Rather, it is a group that embraces certain collective obligations for student success and well-being and that develops a certain collective expertise by employing problem solving, critique, reflection, and debate. In an "emerging framework for analyzing school-based professional community," Kruse, Louis, and Bryk (1995) identify shared values, focus on student learning, reflective dialogue, collaboration, and "deprivatization" of practice as characteristics of professional community. Those characteristics, they argue, are in turn supported by certain *structural* conditions of time, space, responsibility, communication, and decision-making autonomy and by *cultural* or human resource conditions that include openness to improvement, access to expertise, trust and respect, supportive leadership, and socialization of new members.

Consistent with the emerging portrait of teacher learning community, communication maps in "collaborative" schools would show a higher density of communication focused specifically on teaching and learning. Teachers would more often communicate about the progress of students, develop curriculum or assessments together, and spend time in one another's classrooms. Their week would incorporate regularly scheduled time for consultation and collaboration in addition to personal planning time. One might expect to find experienced teachers routinely observing and co-planning with beginning teachers, or teachers at a grade level comparing examples of student writing, or members of an interdisciplinary group trying to determine authentic links between subjects. Links to the outside would be common, and school resources would subsidize teachers' participation in networks, special projects, teacher research, or partnership arrangements.

The larger the school, the more likely it is that all of these portraits apply in some degree. Overall, the prospects for school improvement grow as schools take deliberate steps to reduce the isolation of teachers and to build professional communication that is both intensive and extensive. Along the path from isolation are several possibilities worth cultivating— steady support for individual explorations, reason and opportunity for small collaborations, and a schoolwide environment conducive to teacher learning.

Extending Communication and Collaboration

From the wider array of structural and cultural supports for collaboration and professional community, I have distilled three for close attention. These are conditions that lend themselves in part to formal decision making at the school level, but that also require concerted leadership and consistent "culture building."

Shared Interests and Shared Responsibility (Interdependence)

Professionals are more likely to collaborate when they have a problem that can't be solved, a goal that can't be achieved, or an interest that can't be satisfied by individuals working on their own. Meaningful collaboration arises out of genuine interests or purposes held in common. Teachers may find reason to work together or to learn from one another because they teach similar subjects, grade levels, or students or because they teach in similar circumstances. "Interdependence" at the school level is most evident when teachers share responsibility for the same students, but this need not mean teaching in the same classroom. For example, an elementary school has committed itself to a goal that students will read fluently and confidently by the end of third grade. To ensure that the responsibility does not fall on a few third-grade teachers, teachers in the primary grades have begun meeting regularly to look at samples of student work, talk about what it means to "read fluently and confidently," examine instructional alternatives, and develop solutions to problems. Over time, with one another's help, they may elect to remain with a single cohort of students from first to third grade (turning to each other for materials and ideas for each grade level) or they may attempt multi-age classes learning with each other and from examples outside their school).

Questions to Ask About a School. What shared problems, goals, or interests bring teachers together? Where do teachers find colleagues whose interests most closely intersect with their own (understanding that it may be in other schools)? What do teachers stand to accomplish or learn from and with one another?

Opportunity

Opportunity is the necessary complement to interdependence. Without opportunity to pursue professional contacts, shared interest or responsibility easily breeds frustration. Absent the motivating interest or need, teachers may find "opportunity" meaningless.

Schools create opportunity for professional exchange principally by expanding the amount of discretionary (out-of-classroom) time available to teachers. Schools differ, sometimes dramatically, in the amount and concentration of out-of-class time available to teachers during the salaried week and year. In principle, American schools would do well to support more out-of-class time for teachers. Without altering the number of paid teacher days or lengthening the official duty day, many "restructuring" schools have reorganized time to enable teachers to collaborate on a daily or weekly basis. Elementary schools have "banked" time on 4 days to gain a minimum release day once a week. Secondary schools have organized prep times to join teachers who have reason to work together and have reallocated blocks of faculty meeting time to ensure that departments, cross-subject teams, and special task forces all have the time needed for substantive work together.

Making a productive habit of "team meeting" or "consultation" times proves difficult unless teachers have both reason and time to meet daily or nearly so. Out-of-classroom time has a large appetite, and there is much in the everyday experience of schools to feed it. Among the five "restructured" schools profiled by Louis and Kruse (1995) and their colleagues, only two organized time in ways that promoted professional community.

Apart from providing time for focused consultation and collaboration, schools also shape the time and space for teachers to see each other more informally and to see each other at work with students. Teachers' lounges range from the stark to the welcoming. Whole-school faculty meetings range from substantive discussions to a laundry list of announcements. Outside the occasional drama production, music performance, art display, science fair, or athletic context, teachers rarely have occasion to see the products of each other's classroom effort or see one another directly at work with students. Were teachers more commonly in touch with one another's classroom work, the "stuff" of professional communication might be richer, deeper, and more highly valued.

Questions to Ask About a School. How are time and space configured to support frequent and focused communication among teachers and to permit periods of extended collaboration? What other opportunities do teachers have to communicate and consult with colleagues and others outside the school? What opportunities do teachers have to be in each other's presence informally or to see each other at work with students?

Resources

Until recently, professional communication among teachers during the ordinary school day depended largely on the opportunity for face-to-face contact. With greater frequency, teachers enjoy access to telephones in the classroom and to electronic mail networks. Beyond these rudimentary supports for communication, professional exchange thrives on access to other material resources and to diverse and valued sources of expertise. Even when schools are richly supplied with resources for students (and often they are not), teachers may find themselves insulated from useful information, stimulating alternatives, a range of competing ideas, and productive criticism. Staff lounges or workrooms, school libraries, and team or department offices sometimes provide resources ranging from professional books and journals to Internet access, but more often they are relatively barren. Material resources constitute an investment in teacher knowledge.

Questions to Ask About a School. What resources do teachers have readily available to add to their stock of knowledge and ideas? What preparation and support do teachers receive for making good use of new technologies?

The Troubles That Colleagues Encounter

Even granted the conditions outlined above, teachers might anticipate other challenges to effective collaboration. Here are two that center on within-school conditions. The first—problems that groups encounter with collaboration—calls for a certain willingness to persist in the face of difficulty, aided by specific support in establishing group process and problem-solving strategies. The second—workload obstacles—calls for organizational policies and practices that plausibly support increased communication and collaboration among teachers without generating overload and burnout.

Problems With Collaboration and Communication

For all the benign imagery often attached to words like "collaboration," teachers' stories abound with tales of difficulty and disappointment. A few common problems stand out: disagreements over basic issues of teaching and learning, negotiating a balance between collaboration and autonomy, the tricky divide between "making a suggestion" and "telling someone what to do," jealousies and resentments surrounding individuals or groups, and inadequate knowledge and confidence needed to make working with colleagues at least as effective as working alone.

"Like-mindedness" seems the most likely basis for most collaboration. In the school context, however, teachers may find themselves sharing responsibilities without sharing views of teaching and learning. Close collaborations (e.g., of the sort we find in interdisciplinary teams) bring fundamental beliefs to the surface and may reveal points of deep disagreement. Personal and professional relationships suffer strain when teachers must wrestle with competing beliefs and practices. Even where such factions do not seem evident, we find teachers backing off when they uncover deeply felt differences regarding curriculum priorities and standards for student work. Researchers following the progress of interdisciplinary teams report that

> in their effort to form communities of teacher learners . . . the affective costs associated with conflict and argument comprise important disincentives to teachers' participation. Teachers remark that the personal costs of exposing beliefs, disagreeing with a colleague, having to justify a position, outweigh the benefits they perceive. (McLaughlin & Talbert, in press, describing work under way by Grossman & Wineberg)

For teachers to engage seriously in professional communication with their colleagues, they must be able to initiate open and critical discussions of instruction. Mentoring and advising must constitute an accepted and valued aspect of school life. Staff must be able to put forward new ideas and critically evaluate ideas as they are tried out in practice, but also live with one another through the messiness of discovery. In doing so, they must find factors other than personality differences to explain the difficulties they are having and must also contend with well-documented reluctance to offer advice, express concerns openly, or examine the roots of disagreement.[2]

Overall, collaboration is more likely to yield benefits when it is informed by knowledge of three sorts: substantive knowledge that improves the quality of ideas, plans, and solutions; process knowledge that makes a group effective as a group; and interdisciplinary teams that, for example, bring fundamental beliefs to the surface and may reveal points of deep disagreement.

Workload Problems, or Too Much of a Good Thing

Teachers in small, teacher-controlled partnerships manage to work out the workload possibilities—how much collaboration they will undertake and how much in-school and out-of-school time it will consume. Expectations for communication and formal collaboration tend to increase in a school with the onset of shared decision making or other schoolwide improvement initiatives. Teachers may feel that they are losing control of the focus and scope of collaboration—everything is cast as being "meetinged to death." Administrators and colleagues who witness individuals' efforts to set priorities and regain control over time may interpret it as "resistance." Ambitious school reform activity breeds not only teacher renewal but also teacher burnout. Reducing the probability of burnout requires, in part, that teachers be relieved of overload and supported in concentrating collaboration where it counts most.

Conclusion

At the very least, one must imagine schools in which teachers are in frequent conversation with each other about their work, have easy and necessary access to each other's classrooms, take it for granted that they should comment on each others work, and have the time to develop common standards for student work. (Meier, 1992, p. 602)

In these words, Deborah Meier envisions the professional environment conducive to "reinventing teaching." This chapter presents a highly condensed framework for examining the professional relationships characteristic of a school and for assessing the conditions that foster or impede collaboration. Missing, of course, are the specific histories and contexts that give nuance to each school workplace and that shape the possibilities and limitations of change. This framework may help teachers and administrators to make the possibilities visible; to purse them fully will require curiosity, tenacity, and inventiveness. Pursuit begins with talk about teaching.

Notes

1. In the descriptions that follow, the "isolating" school is most widely associated with Lortie's (1975) analysis of teaching conditions. The "independent artisan" model is based most directly on the work of Huberman (1993), but also draws from work by Flinders (1988) and Hargreaves (1993). To characterize schools that foster a "collaborative culture" or "teacher learning," I have drawn principally on my own work and the work of Louis and Kruse (1995); McLaughlin and Talbert (in press); and Nias, Southworth, and Yeomans (1989); I have also taken account of various ethnographic accounts (such as Metz, 1978) and theories of school micropolitics (Ball, 1987; Blase, 1991) to anticipate the possibility of a "divided" or "balkanized" school.

2. Group problem-solving strategies include diagnosing the sources of apparent group failure (problems with the nature of the task, the group's authority, competing interests, available knowledge and skill, etc.). Ambivalence about advice and helping or about public dissent is not unique to

teaching. There is an extensive body of social-psychological research on this matter. I have summarized parts of it elsewhere (Little, 1990a) to explain some of the difficulties encountered in my formal mentoring programs (see also Glidewell, Tucker, Todt, & Cox, 1983).

References and Resources

The following readings expand the arguments summarized in this brief overview. Only a few have been directly cited in the text. I have tried to keep the list concise and to concentrate on published sources readily available to American educators.

Ball, S. J. (1987). *The micro-politics of the school: Towards a theory of school organization.* London: Methuen.

Blase, J. (Ed.). (1991). *The politics of life in schools: Power, conflict, and cooperation.* Newbury Park, CA: Corwin.

Bruckerhoff, C. (1991). *Between classes: Faculty life at Truman High.* New York: Teachers College Press.

Darling-Hammond, L. (in press). *Beyond bureaucracy: Reinventing schools for learner-centered practice.* San Francisco: Jossey-Bass.

Feiman-Nemser, S., & Floden, R. (1986). The cultures of teaching. In M. Wittrock (Eds.), *Handbook of research on teaching* (3rd ed., pp. 505-526). New York: Macmillan.

Flinders, D. J. (1988). Teacher isolation and the new reform. *Journal of Curriculum and Supervision, 4*(1), 17-29.

Glidewell, J. C., Tucker, S., Todt, M., & Cox, S. (1983). Professional support systems: The teaching profession. In A. Nadler, J. Fisher, & B. DePaulo (Eds.), *New directions in helping* (pp. 189-212). New York: Academic Press.

Hargreaves, A. (1991). Contrived collegiality: The micropolitics of teacher collaboration. In J. Blase (Ed.), *The politics of life in schools: Power, conflict, and cooperation.* Newbury Park, CA: Corwin.

Hargreaves, A. (1993). Individualism and individuality: Reinterpreting the teacher culture. In J. W. Little & M. W. McLaughlin (Eds.), *Teachers' work: Individuals, colleagues, and contexts* (pp. 51-76). New York: Teachers College Press.

Hill, D. (1995). The strong department: Building the department as a learning community. In L. S. Siskin & J. W. Little (Eds.), *The subjects in question: Departmental organization and the high school* (pp. 123-140). New York: Teachers College Press.

Huberman, M. (1993). The model of the independent artisan in teachers' professional relations. In J. W. Little & M. W. McLaughlin (Eds.), *Teachers' work: Individuals, colleagues, and contexts* (pp. 11-25). New York: Teachers College Press.

Kruse, S. D., Louis, K. S., & Bryk, A. S. (1995). An emerging framework for analyzing school-based professional community. In K. S. Louis, S. D. Kruse, & Associates (Eds.), *Professionalism and community: Perspectives on reforming urban schools* (pp. 23-42). Thousand Oaks, CA: Corwin.

Lee, V. E., & Smith, T. (1996). Collective responsibility for learning and its effects on gains in achievement and engagement for early secondary school students. *American Journal of Education, 104*(2), 103-147.

Lieberman, A. (Ed.). (1988). *Building professional culture in schools.* New York: Teachers College Press.

Lieberman, A., & McLaughlin, M. W. (1992). Networks for educational change: Powerful and problematic. *Phi Delta Kappan, 73*(9), 673-677.

Little, J. W. (1982). Norms of collegiality and experimentation: Workplace conditions of school success. *American Educational Research Journal, 19*(3), 325-340.

Little, J. W. (1987). Teachers as colleagues. In V. Richardson-Koehler (Ed.), *Educators' handbook: A research perspective* (pp. 491-518). New York: Longman.

Little, J. W. (1990a). The mentor phenomenon and the social organization of teaching. *Review of Research in Education, 16,* 297-351.

Little, J. W. (1990b). The persistence of privacy: Autonomy and initiative in teachers professional relations. *Teachers College Record, 4,* 509-536.

Little, J. W., & McLaughlin, M. W. (Eds.). (1993). *Teachers' work: Individuals, colleagues, and contexts.* New York: Teachers College Press.

Lortie, D. (1975). *Schoolteacher.* Chicago: University of Chicago Press.

Louis, K. S., & Kruse, S. D. (1995). *Professionalism and community: Perspectives on reforming urban schools.* Thousand Oaks, CA: Corwin.

McLaughlin, M. W., & Talbert, J. E. (in press). *Professional communities and the work of high school teaching.* Chicago: University of Chicago Press.

Meier, D. (1992). Reinventing teaching. *Teachers College Record, 93*(4), 594-609.

Metz, M. H. (1978). *Classrooms and corridors: The crisis of authority in secondary schools.* Berkeley: University of California Press.

Newmann, F., & Wehlage, G. (1995). *Successful school restructuring: A report to the public and educators.* Madison: Center on Organization and Restructuring of Schools, Wisconsin Center for Education Research, University of Wisconsin.

Nias, J., Southworth, G., & Yeomans, R. (1989). *Staff relationships in the primary school: A study of organizational cultures.* London: Cassell.

Rosenholtz, S. (1989). *Teachers' workplace.* New York: Longman.

Siskin, L. S. (1994). *Realm of knowledge: Academic departments in secondary schools.* London: Falmer.

Smylie, M. A. (1994). Redesigning teachers' work: Connections to the classroom. In L. Darling-Hammond (Ed.), *Review of research in education* (Vol. 20, pp. 129-177). Washington, DC: American Educational Research Association.

CHAPTER 5

Teacher Use of Formal Assessment in the Classroom

Eva L. Baker

University of California, Los Angeles
National Center for Research on Evaluation,
Standards, and Student Testing (CRESST)

Teachers have always made judgments about the accomplishments of their students as part of their regular work. These judgments have been made based on methods as diverse as student recitation, review of homework, evaluation of classroom discussion, observation of behavior, test performance, and analyses of student projects. Growing over the past 10 or so years has been concern about how teachers make these judgments about their students' competencies. The issues underlying the renewed emphasis on teacher use of assessment in the classroom relate both to broad policy concerns and to the technical and professional development needed to strengthen teachers' efforts in this area.

In the policy arena, a key impetus for concern about teachers' use of test information is the prevailing belief about the competitiveness of U.S. students in comparative, international studies of achievement. U.S. students are not performing well in these comparisons. On the national level, studies of student performance in the National Assessment of Educational

AUTHOR'S NOTE: The work reported herein was supported under the Educational Research and Development Centers Program, PR/Award Number R305B60002, as administered by the Office of Educational Research and Improvement, U.S. Department of Education. The findings and opinions expressed herein do not reflect the positions and policies of the National Institute on Student Achievement, Curriculum, and Assessment, the Office of Educational Research and Improvement, or the U.S. Department of Education.

Progress report that most students are failing to achieve proficiency. Similarly, when the SAT used for college admissions by a large number of postsecondary institutions needed to be "recentered," or adjusted to reflect lower averages, another question was raised about student performance. In state assessments created to measure curriculum goals and standards, most states also report that many students are achieving below expectation. Colleges and universities enroll ever-increasing numbers of under-prepared students who have met admission standards. Business and industry leaders complain that they must mount expensive training programs to prepare new hires for entry-level positions. There are numerous counterexamples that argue that students today are performing as well as ever and that expectations have risen just as the students we teach have grown more diverse. Nonetheless, the consistency of information and of beliefs about inadequate student achievement from a wide variety of sources has given rise to educational reforms on the local, state, and national level.

One obvious question is whether teachers have similarly detected poor performance in their own classrooms. Teachers' summative judgments, corresponding to external tests such as state assessments, are encapsulated in the grades they give students. Judging from general reports of grade inflation, the answer seems to be that inadequate student performance is not reflected in teachers' grading practices. Without getting sidetracked by a discussion of the utility of grades and their motivational effect or alternatives to conventional grading practices, let us turn to the practical consequences of external testing information that conflicts with summative teacher judgment. One direct response of policymakers has been to seek to assist teachers to be more effective in the judgments they make about students. One strategy is to improve their use of tests and of test results.

There are three additional reasons that teacher testing practices are of interest—fairness, effectiveness, and efficiency. In the case of fairness, there are questions about the meaning and consistency of grades from classroom to classroom and from school to school. When the population of students was similar from school to school, no one was much concerned about variations between stricter or more lenient grading by teachers; any differences were expected to average out. Now that many urban schools deal almost exclusively with disadvantaged students, it is important to document that grading standards are fair, with no particular group of students getting special advantage. This assumption of fairness is needed to ensure the meaningfulness of high school diplomas and for making comparative judgments based on students' grades, for example, in college admissions procedures.

The effectiveness and efficiency arguments relating to teacher testing practices have far less to do with grading and what is called *summative evaluation* and much more to do with helping all students attain their maximum level of performance. *Formative evaluation* is the technical term that describes the use of test results to improve teaching practice and student learning. The purpose of such tests—for instance, those given weekly or monthly—is to identify areas needing additional attention or effort as well as to provide evidence of progress and accomplishments. The use of test results in this case is intended to improve the learning of students who were tested by involving (a) students in reflecting on their work, (b) parents for appropriate assistance, and (c) teachers who would need to undertake additional approaches to help students reach academic goals. Considering instructional improvement in longer cycles, it is reasonable for an instructional team to look at the performance of fourth-grade students in 1999-2000 and take into account their areas of weaknesses when planning for the 2000-2001 school year. This type of formative evaluation provides information to the teaching staff. At the core of these uses is suspicion that teachers may not see student performance as malleable and may attribute all poor performance to factors outside the instructional setting. Consequently, teachers might be more likely to accept results as the best that could have been achieved—instead of analyzing findings and making changes in instructional practices that might contribute to some improvement.

These analyses are not presented as an assertion of their truth but rather to offer an explanation for the attention given to test data in general and teachers' use of test results in particular. Were U.S. students performing well in international comparisons and other external test results and were all teachers highly respected as professionals, such discussions would be markedly less likely.

Improving the Use of Classroom Tests

To improve classroom use of tests, five basic properties of the assessment should be considered: (a) The assessment must be valid, (b) it must be fair, (c) it must be credible, (d) it must be practical, and (e) it must generate useful results. Let us briefly consider each of these properties.

Validity is a concept that means the test measures the aspect (or construct) of student performance of interest. For example, if a good writer can get a high score on a history essay knowing very little history, the test would not be a valid measure of the student's understanding of history. The wrong inference would be drawn from the data. If a student who can do complex mathematics fails a math test because the word problems are written in an unfamiliar language, the test would not be a valid measure of mathematics for that student. Validity also has to do with test content, particularly if the test includes or excludes content that it would be expected to measure. For example, a test involving literary devices that excluded similes would have its validity challenged by English teachers who believe that similes represent an essential component of that content area. Validity also has to do with the purpose of the test. Certain tests may be very good for identifying the best or worst students in a class but not very good for providing diagnostic information. When tests are discussed or proposed, it is always a good idea to raise a question about how the validity of the test has been investigated, for what types of students, and for what particular purposes or uses.

Fairness, our second major element, undergirds much of American values and is an extremely important part of testing practice. Most simply, the precept of fairness means that students should receive examination scores that reflect their particular level of expertise and are free of influences based on group membership, such as gender, language group, or cultural background. Of course, the concept of fairness also implies that the "rules" for preparing, administering, and scoring a test were followed and that scores were not influenced by cheating, inappropriate practice, or unacceptable hints, for instance. Scores should not be influenced by students' background, their differential familiarity with the method of testing, or the use of scoring practices that favor one type of student over another. Because fairness is so important, it is a primary justification for using tests that can be scored objectively.

A third important attribute of tests is their credibility to relevant parties. *Credibility* means the extent to which a test is perceived to be worthwhile and its results to be trusted. If tests are not credible to teachers, they will not be administered, or if mandated, their results will not be taken seriously. If tests have low credibility with students, many may not try hard and their results will not be good measures of the real level of their accomplishments. If tests are not credible to parents and the public, their results will be dismissed as meaningless, and efforts will be made to change the tests to be more in line with public expectations.

The *practicality* of a test refers to the ease of its use in regular classroom settings. If a test is discretionary and also not practical, it will not be used at all or not be used for long. If a test is required and not practical, in that, for example, it takes too much time or requires special materials not easily available or managed, then unforeseen and different adjustments in administration procedures might be made in classrooms that could well invalidate the results.

Finally, classroom tests need to generate results that are *useful*. Tests that give teachers an overall estimate—that students do well or poorly—are less desirable than tests that give guidance about specific topics or skills that need improvement. But more detail is not always better. The level of detail must match the ability of the teacher to make use of the information. For instance, teachers are unlikely to be able to make use of highly refined test results in situations where limited instructional materials are available. For teachers to make very detailed test results useful in planning for each student in a class, there must be deep resources in teachers' personal repertoires or school curriculum and teaching assets.

Two developments that are part of the current educational reform movement may help teachers to use student results in more effective ways. The first is the development in almost every state of "standards" to guide instruction and testing. One kind of standards focuses on the identification of important goals in content to be achieved at various grade levels or age ranges. Some states and districts have identified standards to be met for every grade, whereas others have chosen important points in student development (e.g., at the end of primary education, at the end of elementary school, at the beginning of high school, and at high school graduation). In most cases, these standards bear remarkable resemblance to what used to be called curriculum goals, curriculum guidelines, or frameworks and are intended to describe what students should be expected to accomplish. They are often phrased in a general way—"Students should apply linear and geometric measurement principles to real-life problems"—and then may be augmented by more explicit content specifications, for instance, types of included polygons, to provide further guidance. For the most part, states and districts have reviewed model content standards prepared by national groups focused in particular subject matters, such as those of the National Council of Teachers of Mathematics or the National Science Foundation. In a second part of this standards reform, "performance standards," content standards are made more explicit either by describing a type of task students would be expected to do (estimate distances on a baseball field through geometric methods) or by describing the expectations for performance (answers should be expressed in x units and procedures used should be explained in enough detail that another student could complete them).

These standards are intended to provide guidance for determining both the kinds of learning students should be encouraged to experience and the types of examinations that should be given to students. In the purest form, standards-based assessments would provide a coherent framework for teaching and learning. What is particularly interesting about this cycle of educational reform is its emphasis on high standards for all students. Not since the Sputnik era, where once before international competition was a major impetus for reform, have experts in subject matter provided what are called "challenging" goals for students and educational systems.

A second important component of this round of reform is the emphasis on assessments that map to standards. Many of the standards require students to complete tasks that involve multiple days, multiple steps, and collaboration. The type of assessment most appropriate to measure many of these more complex standards is performance-based assessment. Performance-based assessment is an important initiative because in addition to assessing statements of standards, it is based on the idea that assessment must be like student learning. This simple idea turns on its head the more familiar idea of "alignment," that student learning needs to match the methods used in testing. Because of its deep dependence on learning as psychologists and researchers have come to understand it, performance assessments have certain characteristics. Students are expected to *construct* their answers, because research in learning suggests such constructions are the way students acquire meaning. Students may be asked to perform tasks that have multiple steps, acquiring knowledge or determining the next operation based on the results of a prior activity or prior knowledge. Students may occasionally work in groups because collaboration has been shown to be an important approach for many learners. The consequences of these attributes are performance assessments that take considerable time (no more 2-minute test items), that require judgments or raters to determine level of performance (no more answer key), and that use language as the basis for explaining how and why problems were solved rather than simply inspecting solutions. The time these performance assessments take inevitably limits the number than can be administered in any one subject area, in interdisciplinary topics, or to any one student. The cost of ratings by judges also limits the number of performance assessments that can be administered. Consequently, it is not feasible for the educational system to assess the attainment of all of the standards it seeks to achieve. So it will be expected that teachers will use their own classroom examinations or other methods to assess many of the standards.

How Can Teachers Use Standards-Based Performance Assessments in Their Own Classrooms?

Ideally, professional development will help teachers organize the way they go about their assessment job, and research has shown that it takes considerable time, energy, and knowledge of subject matter to do a good job with performance assessments. A simple set of guidelines may help people get under way. First, determine which standards are being measured by external means, through the use of district or state assessments, commercially available tests, and so on. Seek to acquire whatever you can that specifies the content to be assessed (expanded content standards) or the type of measures and student expectations in the assessments to be administered (performance standards). One source of classroom examinations should be based on components or comparable measures that will be used externally to evaluate the students and the school. For example, if students are expected to use particular procedures in solving mathematics problems, such as a number line, you should develop a classroom assessment that in part uses the same general procedures. Second, determine which standards have been articulated that are impractical for the education system to measure formally. Progress toward these standards can be examined by using your own personal examination procedures. There are numerous models available for the design of performance assessments. One used for a variety of districts and states at the National Center for Research on Evaluation, Standards, and Student Testing (CRESST) creates specifications for each type of learning to be measured and then uses the same general approach in different subject matters. Figure 5.1 shows the five key types of learning CRESST has identified. Most goals (and relevant assessments) in schools are made up of a combination of these learning types, in the same way as an individual's DNA is made up of different combinations of genes.

For each of these areas, at least one set of specifications for guiding performance assessments has been developed. These specifications include the types of materials provided to students, the administration procedures, and the scoring criteria or rubric. For example, in the area of problem solving, the specifications provide a number of choices for the assessment team. They might choose to focus on problems that have multiple right answers or single right answers. The goals of interest might emphasize problems that are clearly formulated. As a comparison, the focus of the assessment could be problems that are complicated and need further clarification. Whether students are provided with all the information necessary

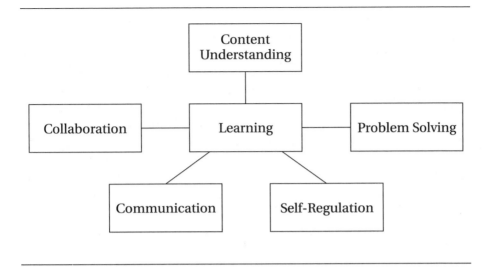

Figure 5.1: CRESST Model of Learning-Based Assessment

to solve the problem, are expected to have already acquired the information, or are provided opportunity to seek relevant information (e.g., in their books, in the library, or on the Internet) are other choices. Performance in problem solving can use criteria related to problem identification, strategy selection, use of prior knowledge, and fluency. It should be clear that such components in scoring criteria not only encompass important attributes of problem solving (documented in the research literature) but provide areas that teachers can address in both initial and any continuing instruction to assist students in acquiring competence.

What is most important about the problem-solving model as it has been formulated is that its structure can be applied to different subject matter areas, for instance, social studies, mathematics, and science. Thus a teacher or assessment team need only learn well the specifications (or create their own) and apply them to multiple subjects taught in the classroom or school. Specifications have been widely used in the area of content understanding as well, where students are presented with source materials that include relevant content information. Primary source materials are used in history and geography—speeches, letters, films, and maps. In language arts, literature or literary analyses or audiotapes can be used. In science, descriptions, write-ups, graphs, or videos of experiments may be provided. In mathematics, problems are provided and alternative strategies or solutions may be given. The students then prepare analyses and explanations of the source materials. So far, two major approaches have been used.

One involves the preparation of a written explanation where the student explains to a friend or relative the key principles involved and explains why the material is important. These explanations are scored using a well-researched approach involving an overall judgment of the student's content understanding and use of principles, prior knowledge, and argument appropriate to the subject matter. These essays are often scored for English writing conventions as well. Another set of specifications related to content understanding uses the same sort of stimulus materials, but permits students either individually or in teams to create graphical depictions of the relationship among key principles and ideas in the form of a concept map. These maps are scored in terms of their fidelity to maps made by an expert or teacher. One recent breakthrough is our ability to score these maps automatically using computer support. Specifications for performance assessments also exist in the areas of collaboration, communication, and self-regulation. The benefit of using this type of approach is its general applicability to multiple subject matters and the relief it provides from reinventing assessment approaches time after time. There is also some evidence that teaching toward one assessment (e.g., in a different topic in history) helps students apply the appropriate analytical process to an assessment on a different topic.

Without doubt, creating one's own performance assessments is a task involving great commitment. But to do so where standards-based reform is under way provides a unique opportunity to integrate two aspects of assessment that have been largely separated from each other: external or accountability-focused assessment and teacher-designed classroom assessment intended to provide feedback and improve learning. If both sorts of assessment can be generated from conceptions of learning that also guide instruction, there is real opportunity to improve the performance of our students in a coherent, sensible way. Integrity of the educational system will ultimately depend on the coincidence of goals, learning, teaching, and assessment. Approaches that attract these elements rather than set them in opposition to one another are essential to the success of our schools.

CHAPTER 6

Assessment as Learning

Lorna M. Earl

Ontario Institute for Studies in Education
University of Toronto

The Times They Are Changing

The 1990s felt like a roller-coaster ride for most teachers and schools. There seems to be no end to the changes (economic, cultural, political, and socioeconomic) that schools are expected to keep up with, or even lead. As Hargreaves (1994) reminds us, "Few people want to do much about the economy, but everyone—politicians, the media, and the public alike—wants to do something about education" (p. 5). The role of education is being hotly debated in boardrooms, living rooms, and staff rooms, and teachers are caught in the middle of what often appear to be conflicting and countervailing demands, struggling to maintain their balance. Nevertheless, teachers are expected to navigate their passage through the unrest and uncertainty about how schools should be organized, what should be taught, how to teach, and how assessment should occur.

Whatever else, it is likely that this chaos will continue in the 21st century, and the success of the culture will rely heavily on having citizens with a host of new literacies—computer, scientific, civic, cultural, and so on. To function productively, all students will need to attain the foundation skills of language and mathematics and a whole range of "new basics" such as accessing, interpreting, and applying information; critical thinking and analysis; solving novel problems; making informed judgments; working independently and in groups; and discerning appropriate courses of action in ambiguous situations.

Traditionally, many students have left school to become part of an uneducated or undereducated lower class. In the world of the future, society cannot afford to squander or waste this human potential. We are entering an era where the goal of schooling is to educate all children well, rather than selecting a "talented tenth" to be prepared for knowledge work (Darling-Hammond, 1994). It is no longer sufficient for schools to sort their students and cull out the ones who don't fit the school's recipe for learning. Instead, learning is becoming the fundamental purpose of schooling. This is a dramatic change in the assumptions underlying education and it requires a different view of schools, schooling, teachers, teaching, and, particularly, assessment. In this conception, *schools* have the responsibility for preparing *all* students for tomorrow's world; *teachers* have the wherewithal to guide all students to high levels of learning; and *assessment,* first and foremost, is part of student learning.

Classroom Assessment—Serious Stuff

This chapter is about classroom assessment—the kind of assessment that happens in classrooms, by teachers. Certainly large-scale assessment that is done by the district or state is important; but the really meaningful assessment is done by teachers. As Stiggins (1990) noted, "The assessments that drive student learning and academic self-worth are those used in classrooms" (p. 1). Classroom assessment is the basis for decisions that teachers make about things such as what to teach and to whom, what to communicate to parents, and who to promote to the next grade. It is the basis for decisions that students make as well—about such things as their sense of personal accomplishment; their feelings of self-worth; their willingness to engage in the academic work of schools (e.g., whether to do schoolwork, what schoolwork to do, and with whom they are likely to do schoolwork); and, ultimately, the value that they attach to education.

Teachers intuitively trust their own classroom assessments, prefer them to other assessment methods, and use them for instructional purposes and for determining students' grades (Rogers, 1991; Stiggins, 1994). Unless they are under close public scrutiny, schools and teachers pay little attention to externally imposed tests and go about their own business, using classroom assessment for their judgments (Brown, 1989). They believe that their own assessments and observations are direct, unmediated, and inherently valid, unlike external tests, which, they argue, are indirect, mediated, and inherently invalid (Broadfoot, 1994; Wilson, 1994).

Classroom assessment can be one of the most powerful levers for enhancing student learning. It can be a risky business, however, because it is neither straightforward nor rational. Assessment is a deeply personal and emotional experience for the student being assessed, for the student's parents, and often for the teacher too (Earl & LeMahieu, 1997). It is spontaneous, idiosyncratic, unpredictable, context dependent, time constrained, and group influenced and leads to different responses depending on the student involved (Wilson, 1994), and it is constrained by state, district, and school policies that require particular kinds of reporting or attach rewards or sanctions to student grades (Darling-Hammond, 1994).

Even though classroom assessment is the method of choice for most teachers, there are many problems with existing classroom assessment practices. These problems are not trivial, particularly because classroom assessment can have far-reaching consequences for students.

- *Competing Purposes.* Teachers use assessment for many different purposes, such as classifying and selecting students, planning instruction, assigning grades, reporting to parents, certifying accomplishments, diagnosing student learning, facilitating learning, clarifying course expectations, and motivating and controlling student behavior (Natriello, 1987; Stiggins, 1994; Wilson, 1994). Many of these purposes are inherently incompatible, and teachers have difficulty distinguishing their purposes and being sure that their assessments match the purposes.

- *Assessment Illiteracy.* As schools change and as assessment demands become more complex, teachers are left with the sinking feeling that they don't know enough to implement new models of assessment. Most of them have had little formal training in assessment, and even those who have had training find that is not very useful in their work (McLean, 1985). As a result, fundamental measurement theory is missing in most classrooms (Wilson, 1990). As Stiggins (1991) describes it, teachers are caught in a curious paradox: "We are a nation of assessment illiterates . . . educators and non-educators alike are not sufficiently literate in the basics of assessment to know whether or their achievement data are sound or unsound" (p. 535).

- *"Standards Stew."* Teacher's judgments, as they are expressed in marks and grades, are most often a mishmash of content knowledge and skills, judged in relation to an undefined group (the class, or all classes this term, or all the classes I have taught over the years), and finally adjusted based on idiosyncrasies that exist for this particular student (attends class, works hard, polite). The shifting ingredients in the stew make it difficult for anyone other than the teacher involved to disentangle the pieces and make meaning out of the resulting symbolic representation as a number or letter grade.

Assessment as Learning

Classroom assessment should not be abandoned nor replaced because of its difficulties. Instead, it should be transformed, strengthened, and focused so that it becomes a powerful instrument of learning for students and also for teachers.

Historically, tests, quizzes, projects, and so on have occurred at or near the end of instruction, as a basis for reporting to parents and making selection or placement decisions. Assessments differentiated or sorted students into groups and, in the process, set or confirmed their future schooling, their likely employment, and the course of their lives. This process worked well enough for most students and largely went unchallenged, as long as there were plenty of places for the majority of students to lead productive and worthwhile lives, many of which did not depend directly on passing or failing in school (e.g., agriculture, manufacturing, trades). As the world has changed, this approach is proving to be inadequate. High school graduation is a minimum prerequisite for almost all jobs; students and their parents are refusing to accept the judgment of educators as fair, especially when the criteria for the judgments are vague or kept secret and the result is that some receive status and opportunity and are valued, while others are excluded or diminished. At the same time, we are learning a great deal about how people learn. The human mind is a fascinating but mysterious organ. So much about how it works is still unknown. Teachers, as the guides of the mind, have a responsibility to remain ever vigilant for new knowledge about learning and to continually rethink their approach to teaching and their assessment practices in relation to learning theory.

Imagine a different conception of assessment, one that is rooted in the far past, one that holds assessment as an inextricable part of learning. It is ironic that the word *assessment* is derived form the Latin word *assidere*—"to sit with" (Wiggins, 1993). Its very origin implies more than marks, percentiles, grade point averages, and cut scores. It also suggests a perspective that eschews efficiency and economy as assessment hallmarks. Instead, it conjures up images of teachers observing students, talking with them, and working with them to unravel their understandings and misunderstand-ings—making assessment an integral part of learning that offers detailed feedback to the teacher and the student (Earl & LeMahieu, 1997).

This notion of *assessment as learning* is deeply rooted in a construc-tivist theory that learning is a process of taking in information; interpreting it; connecting it to existing knowledge or beliefs; and, if necessary, reorga-nizing understanding to accommodate the new information (Shepard, 1991). If people learn by constructing their own understanding from their experiences, assessment is not only part of learning, it is the critical compo-nent that allows learners (and teachers) to check their understanding against the views of others and against the collective wisdom of the culture as it has been recorded in the knowledge, theories, models, formulas, solu-tions, and stories that make up the curriculum and the disciplines. The no-tion that assessment is inextricably tied to learning challenges the very core of many educational practices and raises the specter for teachers of funda-mentally changing much of what they do. This challenge is daunting but seductive, especially for teachers who see teaching as a moral enterprise and the moral purpose of teachers as enhancing or enriching the lives of their students (Fullan, 1993). There is no "one right way" to assess students; rather, teachers have to create their own understanding and make their own professional decisions moment by moment. And there are many excit-ing approaches emerging in classrooms.

Getting There

It won't be a simple task to change assessment in schools. In fact, there will be many vocal opponents to the views that I have described in this chapter. But opposition is not a sufficient reason for refusing to try. The ideas in this section are ones that have been observed, proposed, tried, and adapted by teachers working in all kinds of schools, at all grade levels, and in a variety of places around the world. I offer them here as starting points for some and touchstones for others. Use them for discussion and for action as you ven-ture along or continue on the pathway of assessment as learning.

- *Declare Your Purpose.* If you are using assessment as learning, tell your students. Show them in your actions and your words that this is an exercise in self-discovery for them and that you are their guide, their men-tor, and their mirror. Make them participants in their own learning and pro-vide them with many, many opportunities to use assessment to challenge their own knowledge and beliefs, without the interference of anxiety about marks and class standing.

- *No Surprises.* When students and parents, as well as teachers, understand what is expected of them, they have a much better chance of reaching the expectations. Learning targets should be clear, and descriptions and examples of good work should not only be visible to students and parents but also be open for negotiation and adjustment. Reporting to students and parents should be continuous, reciprocal conversations about progress and about learning, not merely information giving. Judgments should not arrive suddenly, by surprise, when the time for action is far past, but as shared decisions heralding the next steps in learning.

- *Self-Assessment Should Be the Ultimate Goal.* Stiggins (1993) said it all:

  If you want to appear accountable, test your students.

  If you want to improve schools, teach teachers to assess their students.

  If you want to maximize learning, teach students to assess themselves.

Students need to become their own best assessors. A participatory democracy depends on citizens who can make informed and defensible decisions. If students are to become critical thinkers and problem solvers who can bring their talents and knowledge to bear on unanticipated problems, they have to develop high-level skills of self-assessment and self-adjustment. Broadfoot (1994) describes a study in Great Britain in which teachers came to realize that the things that really made a difference in students' motivation and the quality of their learning were (a) sharing and discussing curriculum goals with students, (b) encouraging students to set their own learning targets and make "learning plans," (c) involving students in assessing their own work so that they were more willing and able to monitor their own learning and took greater responsibility for doing so, and (d) teachers and students reviewing progress together and revising "learning plans" based on information from classroom assessments. Effective assessment empowers learners to ask reflective questions and consider many strategies. It is not likely that students will become competent, realistic self-evaluators on their own. They need to be taught skills of self-evaluation and have routine and challenging opportunities to practice and validate their own judgments (Earl & Cousins, 1995).

- *Making Connections.* The essence of assessment as learning for teachers lies in being talented conductors with the complete musical score in their head and a flair for improvisation. They must hear the nuances of each instrument, intuit the emotions of the players, allow them the freedom to experiment, and subtly guide and extend the talent and virtuosity of each of them in personal ways by providing feedback and encouragement moment by moment.

• *Working Together.* As teachers engage in classroom assessment, they are plagued with questions: How sure am I that I'm right? Is this really an accurate and fair picture of this student's learning? These questions become particularly important when teachers' judgments carry serious consequences for students. In measurement terms, these are issues of *reliability* and *validity.* Teachers don't need to know the nuances of these concepts, but they do need to be able to ensure that their assessments are both reliable and valid. One of the most powerful ways to increase confidence in assessments is for teachers to work together and share decision making. When teachers work together to establish criteria for judging their students' work, set standards, locate examples of quality work, and make group decisions, the collaboration has many spin-offs. At the very least, it gives teachers some confidence in their decisions because they did not come to them in isolation. In the long run, they develop agreement about the nature and quality of their assessment and of the students' work. When teachers share the decisions about how to assess, there will be fewer discrepancies in student assessment standards and procedures between grades or classes; they will develop a deeper understanding of curriculum and of individual students; and they will engage in the intense discussions about standards and evidence that lead to a shared understanding of expectations for students, more refined language about children and learning, and consistent procedures for making and communicating judgments. This exercise becomes even more powerful when students are involved in the practice of setting and internalizing standards for their own work.

Classroom assessment matters. I can imagine a time, in the not too, too distant future when it is not viewed with foreboding and terror; not separated from teaching and learning; not used to punish or prohibit access to important information; and not seen as a private, mystical ceremony. Instead, assessment and teaching and learning will be reciprocal, each contributing to the other in ways that enhance both. I believe as Haney (1991) does:

Once teachers begin such efforts, the difficulties fall away and their work becomes, in a sense, easier. They become thoughtful observers, documenters and organizers of evaluation. In the end, these fresh directions are not as complex as they appear. They call upon us to ask, in relation to purpose, what would cause us to say that our students are thinkers, readers, writers and comprehenders of knowledge, and to then work out systematic processes to follow up such questions. In doing so, we make assessment a more powerful educational tool and return credibility to school practice. Most important, though, we improve the quality of student learning. (p. 166)

References and Resources

Broadfoot, P. (1994, October). *Assessment and evaluation: To measure or to learn?* Paper presented at the International Conference on Evaluation, Toronto.

Brown, R. (1989). Testing and thoughtfulness. *Educational Leadership, 46*(7), 31-33.

Darling-Hammond, L. (1994). Performance-based assessment and educational equity. *Harvard Educational Review, 64*(1), 25.

Earl, L., & Cousins, B. (1995). *Classroom assessment: Changing the face; facing the change.* Toronto: Ontario Public School Teachers' Federation.

Earl, L., & LeMahieu, P. (1997). Rethinking assessment and accountability. In A. Hargreaves (Ed.), *Rethinking educational change with heart and mind.* Alexandria, VA: Association for Supervision and Curriculum Development.

Fullan, M. (1993). *Change forces: Probing the depths of educational reform.* London: Falmer.

Haney, W. (1991). We must take care: Fitting assessments to function. In V. Perrone (Ed.), *Expanding student assessment.* Alexandria, VA: Association for Supervision and Curriculum Development.

Hargreaves, A. (1994). *Changing teachers, changing times.* Toronto: Ontario Institute for Studies in Education Press.

McLean, L. (1985). *The craft of student evaluation in Canada.* Toronto: Canadian Education Association.

Natriello, G. (1987). The impact of evaluation processes on students. *Educational Psychologist, 22*(2), 155-175.

Rogers, T. (1991). Educational assessment in Canada. *Alberta Journal of Educational Research, 36*(2), 179-192.

Shepard, L. (1991). Psychometricians' beliefs about learning. *Educational Research, 36*(2), 179-192.

Stiggins, R. (1990). *Understanding the meaning and importance of quality classroom assessment.* Portland, OR: Northwest Regional Laboratory.

Stiggins, R. (1991, March). Assessment illiteracy. *Phi Delta Kappan,* pp. 534-539.

Stiggins, R. (1993, May). *Student-centered assessment.* Workshop sponsored by the Association of Educational Research Officers of Toronto.

Stiggins, R. (1994). *Student-centered classroom assessment.* New York: Merrill.

Wiggins, G. (1993). *Assessing student performance.* San Francisco: Jossey-Bass.

Wilson, R. (1990). Classroom processes in evaluation student achievement. *Alberta Journal of Educational Research, 36*(2), 134-144.

Wilson, R. (1994, May). *Back to basics: A revisionist model of classroom-based assessment.* Paper presented at the annual meeting of the Canadian Educational Research Association, Calgary, Alberta.

CHAPTER 7

Transforming Professional Development
Understanding and Organizing Learning Communities

Ann Lieberman
Carnegie Foundation for the Advancement of Teaching

Lynne Miller
University of Southern Maine

The need for continuous professional development of teachers may be one of the few things that policymakers, researchers, professional associations, the public, and school personnel agree on. But there is widespread disagreement once we begin to ask, what counts as professional development? What matters most to teachers? How can professional development be organized, supported, and sustained to ensure long-term commitment to student learning goals? The reasons for disagreement are multifaceted. It is easy to hire consultants, give workshops, invite speakers, and create more demanding courses of study. Thus districts and states often do the expedient thing. They provide money to create programs, provide more courses, or pay consultants to teach district and school personnel how to enhance their repertoire. This sometimes works when the content is packaged in such a way that it can be adapted to teachers' classroom practice. It is harder to figure out how to mount long-term, collaborative, professional development that is supported by enabling policies shaped by the constituencies involved in renewing schools. But that is precisely what needs to happen. Professional development, rather than being decontextualized from the classroom of teachers, needs to be reconceived as the linchpin of school reform (Darling-Hammond, 1993, Elmore, 1996; Little et al., 1987).

We argue here that the kinds of changes needed in schools and in the relationships between principals, teachers, and their peers—as well as between teachers and their students—demand invention, adaptation, and a new sense of community that has heretofore not been a part of the culture of most schools (Little, 1996, McLaughlin & Talbert, 1993). As Elmore (1996) found in his research, professional development is not "taking back" something to the school, but rather, permeates the work of the school. New practices are created or learned in the school. They are not a fixed menu. Conceiving of professional development as synonymous with building a learning community lends itself to longer-term solutions and imaginative organizational arrangements that transform the very meaning of adult development and the school itself. How is this to happen? And what does research have to offer?

Three bodies of research and practice help us understand the purposes and practices that are involved in thinking about and organizing for a conception of professional development that is rooted in school renewal and the everyday practices of teachers. These are (a) teacher career development and personal change, (b) school organization to support ongoing learning communities, and (c) educational reform networks that support teacher learning.

Teacher Career Development and Personal Change

Teachers function both as individuals and as members of communities. Too often, however, organizational roles and responsibilities are emphasized at the expense of individual concerns and needs. Teachers range in age from their early 20s to mid or late 60s. Like the children they teach, they too pass through different developmental states—from the trying on of new roles in early adulthood to the acceptance of one's mortality in mid and late adulthood. And as in other developmental theories, these stages are not fixed; rather they are suggestive of general patterns. Each stage has its tasks and challenges; some represent periods of balance and stability, whereas others are marked by crisis and disequilibrium (Erikson, 1963; Levinson, 1978). Although men and women pass through similar life stages, they vary in the pace and intensity of their transitions. Childbearing, child rearing, and general caretaking have special significance for women and growing importance to more and more men. For all teachers, personal issues, such as marriage, divorce, childbirth, changes in economic status or needs, and parenting their children and/or parents affect their capacity for commitment and growth.

Individuals also pass through a sequence of career stages. Fessler and Christensen (1992) document the interacting spheres that affect a teacher. These are (a) personal environment, which includes life stages, family, critical incidents, crises, individual dispositions, and avocational outlets; (b) factors in organizational environment such as unions, regulations, management style, public trust, societal expectations, and professional organizations; and (c) position in the career cycle, beginning with preservice education and moving on to induction, competency building, enthusiasm and growth, career stability, career wind-down, and exit.

Huberman's (1995) work, focused extensively on the career cycle, chronicles a teaching career that has five stages. In Years 1 to 3, teachers focus on issues of career entry where survival and discovery are the major concerns. In Years 4 to 6, teachers enter a stage of stabilization, followed in Years 7 to 18 by two paths, one marked by experimentation and diversification and the other by stocktaking and interrogations. In Years 19 to 30, teachers again follow one of two paths. Teachers who have been experimental move into serenity; teachers who chose stocktaking move toward conservatism. At the end of the career cycle, in Years 31 to 40, teachers approach disengagement, which can be serene or bitter depending on teachers' previous paths and choices.

Yet another approach to individual teacher career development focuses on pedagogy (Academy for Educational Development, 1985). In early stages of their careers, teachers focus on the day-to-day problems of management, discipline, instruction, and subject matter. They struggle with the complexity of linking what they have learned to their work in practice. In the next stage, teachers learn the culture of the school and piece together an "instructional program," a personal survival kit that helps them feel more confident but does not lead to personal inquiry. In the third stage, teachers reach a plateau of "generalized pedagogy." They are concerned with providing the best instruction for the most students. Finally, a small number of teachers progress to the stage of "differentiated pedagogy" where they discover fresh routes to effectiveness and consistently adapt instruction and the curriculum to the needs, interest, and abilities of all students.

What accounts for individual growth and development from one stage to another? From less to more sophisticated pedagogy? From stabilization to experimentation and serenity rather than stocktaking and bitterness? How is it that some teachers remain "stuck" while others progress? The research on individual teacher change provides some answers. One response is posed by Loucks-Horsley and Stiegelbauer (1991), who reference over two decades of evidence. They argue that teachers' personal concerns are pivotal to their ability and willingness to adapt and change. When presented with an innovation, teachers pass through seven levels of concern. These are (a) awareness (I am not concerned about it), (b) information (I would like to know more about it), (c) personal (How will using this affect me?), (d) management (I seem to be spending all of my time getting materials ready), (e) consequence (How is my use affecting the students? How can I refine it to have more impact?), (f) collaboration (How can I relate what I am doing to what others are doing?), and (g) refocusing (I have some ideas about something that would work even better). Loucks-Horsley and Stiegelbauer caution that "change is a process, not an event" and teachers must adapt to change personally and developmentally.

Another response to teacher change is offered by Showers, Joyce, and Bennett (1987), who conclude from their research that teachers need access to four conditions if they are to change. First, they must understand the theory or reason behind any change they are asked to make or consider. Second, they must see demonstrations of the changed practice in a real classroom. Third, they must practice the new behaviors associated with the change in an environment that honors and supports risk taking. Finally, they need opportunities for feedback and coaching from colleagues and supervisors. If any of these conditions are not present, the authors argue, teacher change will not take hold and teachers will retreat to old and familiar practices.

Yet another perspective on teacher change is offered by Guskey (1986), who challenges the conventional wisdom that a change in teacher beliefs and attitudes must precede any changes in teacher practice. Guskey's research supports just the opposite relationship. He argues that substantial change in teacher attitudes and beliefs occurs only after teachers have changed their practices and they see the results of these changes in student outcomes. This chain of events is explained, according to Guskey, by the intense relationship teachers have with their students and the connections they make between what they believe and what they see working in their own classrooms.

The research on adult and teacher career development and the processes of teacher change all speak to the need to tie professional development to the specific teachers for whom development is intended. Every staff is a collection of individuals, each with his or her own personal and career history. One size does not fit all; this is as true for teachers as it is for the students they teach. Professional development needs to be developmental and adaptive in its approach. It has to acknowledge the needs and concerns of individuals and the personal connections they make to their classroom work. For instance, the direct teaching model based on a number of inservice days where all teachers learn the same thing at the same time and in the same way must be replaced with particular study groups, action research, or curriculum groups providing teachers with choice, interest, and appropriate experiential levels as well as attending to different needs. One overall general session might be followed by a variety of choices recognizing the different developmental needs of teachers.

Organizing Schools to Support Ongoing Learning Communities

Although teachers are individuals and no two are alike, professional development takes place in particular schools with particular cultures in particular contexts. Little (1993) argues that the dominant "training" model of professional development, which focuses on expanding the skills in a teacher's individual repertoire, is important but may not fit the ambitious visions of reform in teaching and learning. This model must give way to new reform requirements. The new requirements will need to put teachers at the helm, supporting them as full partners in reform. Implementation of particular ideas, Little reminds us, comes not just from a given program but from a professional community of teachers talking about, debating, trying out, inventing solutions in the context of their own departments or grade levels. The complex challenges of reform, which include, in part, agreed-on higher standards, new forms of assessment, pedagogical practices such as more coaching and facilitation, student engagement that is more active, and attention to a wider variety of student learning styles, demand attention to a long-term agenda with numerous entry points. For example, rather than focusing on teaching and teaching behaviors, professional development might focus on student work and allow teachers to see how external standards relate to their classroom practice. There are many tools that use student work as the focus, for example, "the tuning protocol" (a structured way of assessing student work), descriptive review of students (which provides a structured way of looking at a particular child using a teacher group for its insights), or "the slice" (a strategic sampling of student work in one 48-hour period that gives teachers an opportunity to look at how students experience their school program). All these examples actively involve teachers as learners and put the focus on students—probably the most powerful learning experience for teachers.

Although professional development of teacher practice is an individual, personal learning experience, there is growing evidence that teacher learning is most powerful, long lasting, and continuous when it occurs as a result of being a member of a group of colleagues who all struggle together to plan for a given group of students (Lieberman, 1995a, McLaughlin, 1998; Newmann & Wehlage, 1995). Such professional communities reverse the isolation of teachers from one another and replace this isolation with a group of peers working together to connect their students to school and to learning and, in the process, to each other.

As Newmann & Wehlage (1995) report from their 5-year study of 24 schools in the process of restructuring, when schools organize themselves to engage teachers in a community where teachers share a common purpose for student learning, engage in collaborative activity to achieve those purposes, and take collective responsibility for doing so, student learning improves. Similar findings have been reported by McLaughlin and Talbert (1993) in their 5-year study of the contexts of secondary schools. They found that professional learning communities in secondary schools were necessary for teachers to move from traditional "teacher-centered" values to "student-centered" pedagogy. Teachers in learning communities report that they

1. openly discussed their practices with fellow teachers.

2. used different methods with students that were more active.

3. engaged in social relationships that were collegial.

4. blurred the lines of expert and novice, providing a more egalitarian ethos among more experienced and new teachers.

5. collectively built a technical culture that enhanced student learning.

Similar themes have been reported in elementary and middle schools (Battistich, Solomon, Kim, Watson, & Schaps, 1995; Dasho & Kendzior, 1995; Fullan, 1991; Lieberman, 1995a; Newmann & Wehlage, 1995). These studies document a process of change that involves teachers in working together as a group, having experience that is new to them in how to create caring communities, talking about it, learning from it, gaining support from administration, and learning how to deal with the conflict that comes with peers over learning new ways of teaching and learning or confronting conflicting values of pedagogy and practice. New mechanisms to support opportunities for dialogue and keeping the focus on students are often developed. These processes involve teachers in a collective struggle to try different ways of engaging students, and as they do, together, teachers gain confidence in themselves and their colleagues and begin to identify their practice with larger goals for students. Such communities involve as much generation of new knowledge and method as adaptation of curricular and reform ideas. For example, a group of elementary teachers can discuss their experience in keeping students for 2 years rather than 1.

Using teachers' own experiences provides them with opportunities to talk about what they learn from observing and working with children and their families over an extended period of time. This exchange of ideas and experiences places a community of teachers in charge of their own learning. Such communities "are built as teachers, unpacking the baggage of years of unexamined attitudes, beliefs, and practices, come to trust one another enough to participate in group discussions" about their own practices in teaching and learning (Lieberman, 1995b, p. 14).

Professional learning communities for teachers are often organized by teachers with the facilitation of their administrators. Comprehensive change in a school requires focusing on issues of restructuring and transformation of the school rather than on specific projects or innovations. Concerns are less with "cooperative learning" or "interdisciplinary themes" (although these may well be a part of school practice) than with building a school culture that supports teachers and students in a caring community The vision and values concerned with such ideas take root slowly, but the changes they make distinguish these schools—their principals, teachers, and students—from others. These are schools where changed practices focus on active learning for students; changed structures support these practices; and, eventually, a collective focus and a structure to support the focus lead them toward building cultures of colleagueship, continuous inquiry into practice, and collaborative work. For example, one elementary school in southern Maine, after much restructuring of the school, decided on a rotating "teacher-scholar" position—the person filling the role is released from classroom teaching for a year to carry out disciplined inquiry on behalf of the school.

Such professional communities do indeed change professional development from a focus on particular topics to a broad and continually changing agenda that serves the particulars of the school and its community. But schools need outside partners that enlarge their community and their base of support as this provides expanded opportunities for teachers to learn and practice leadership and multiple avenues for the development of teacher commitment.

Educational Reform Networks That Support Teacher Learning

There is increasing evidence that schools that are involved in restructuring their relationships with students and are better meeting their needs are also schools connected to external sources of support (Cushman, 1996; Darling-Hammond & McLaughlin, 1995; Lieberman & Grolnick, 1996; Lieberman & McLaughlin, 1992; Lieberman & Miller, 1990; Little & McLaughlin, 1991; Lord, 1991; McLaughlin & Talbert, 1993; Newmann & Wehlage, 1995). These external supports, whether subject matter collaboratives, reform networks, or school-university partnerships, are coming to play a critical role in the building of learning communities for teachers and are reshaping the meaning of professional development. Perhaps the most successful reform network has been the National Writing Project, which involves teachers in an intense summer institute, deliberately creating teacher-leaders who then go back and create networks among teachers in their own districts.

There is reason to believe that because schools are organized in ways that often do not encourage the kind of frank discussion that is necessary for inventing new modes of working with students, networks are filling this need. Research on networks, partnerships, and coalitions has now begun to document how these new borderless organizations provide a transition or bridge between bureaucratic organizations and the growth of a more professional orientation in schools and districts. These professional communities with their more egalitarian ethos and supportive learning alternatives are helping to give shape to new forms of adult and professional development as they play a mediating role between practice and policy (Lieberman & Grolnick, 1996; McLaughlin, 1998).

Networks as Intentional Learning Communities

Working across districts (or even, in some cases, across states), teachers find it easier to question, ask for help, or "tell it like it is," rather than being fearful that they are exposing their lack of expertise in a given area. Coming together with educators, where their primary identification is that they all work in and with schools, seems to make communication come easier and problem posing legitimate. In fact, although a great deal of reform knowledge may need to be invented by school-based educators, norms that encourage invention are not as yet part of the way most schools and districts operate. Networks, because they are a more flexible organizational form, offer new ways of operating that are more accepting of the way the processes of teaching, learning, and leading really are—ambiguous, complex, unfinished—and thus tend to be more in tune with how school professionals live and view their lives. Teachers find that "just in time" learning that focuses on immediate problems of practice as well as problems of greater complexity are the agenda of reform networks. In addition, these coalitions offer teachers at different life and career stages diverse entry points for their own development. (The Coalition of Essential Schools [CES] provides a fall forum where 3,000 to 5,000 teachers come to learn from one another.) Such an organizational form is not only helpful but offers people membership in a constructive community: a group of professionals engaged together in a common struggle to educate themselves so that they can better educate their students.

Building Commitment Through Flexible and Responsive Activities

Networks have the flexibility to organize activities first and then develop the structures needed to support those activities—thus differing radically from the organizations in which most of us live. (Established formal organizations have structures that are permanent and create activities to fit the structures.) This kind of flexibility allows a network to create an activity, use it as long as it serves the membership's needs and purposes, and end it when it is no longer perceived as valuable. The responsiveness of the network provides for a more developmental approach to adult learning, empowering its members to voice their approval or disapproval, building commitment to the network rather than to a given activity, and encouraging a more personal and professional involvement of members in their own learning. (In the Southern Maine Partnership, "dine and discuss" became associated with the partnership. University and school-based educators came together to discuss articles. After 2 years, members grew tired of the format and suggested getting rid of it. Several years later, it was reinstated when members said "Whatever happened to 'dine and discuss'?")

It is not just the formats for learning that are different, but the very meaning of adult learning itself: Prescription and compliance are replaced by a challenging involvement in problem posing, sharing, and solving; discussions that concern actions and consequences; and a culture that encourages continuous inquiry.

Networks have their problems too. To succeed, they must negotiate artfully between organizing compelling activities and linking them to larger purposes; create activities that combine "inside knowledge" that teachers develop and "outside knowledge" from reformers, researchers, and the professions; organize a small central staff with school-based educators as active participants; guard against formalizing informal relationships and activities that define the network as it expands; and intentionally decide whether membership will be inclusive or exclusive.

We have enough research evidence to suggest that networks, when they link to school reform and active work being accomplished in the school by teachers, form the basis of professional development that is built on norms that attract university, business, and community-based organizations and professional associations. The givens for networks are that they are developmental, adaptive, improvisational, and responsive to the individual and organizational concerns of their members. In their way, they are linking the three areas of research in ways that are reshaping professional development to fit this era of reform.

References and Resources

Academy for Educational Development. (1985). Improving pedagogy: Phases of teacher development. In *Teacher development in schools*. New York: Ford Foundation.

Battistich, V., Solomon, D., Kim, D., Watson, M., & Schaps, E. (1995). Schools as communities, poverty levels of student populations, and students' attitudes, motives, and performance: A multilevel analysis. *American Educational Research Journal, 32*(3), 627-658.

Cushman, K. (1996, September). Networks and essential schools: How trust advances learning. *Horace, 13*(31).

Darling-Hammond, L. (1993). Reframing the school reform agenda: Developing capacity for school transformation. *Phi Delta Kappan, 74*(10), 753-761.

Darling-Hammond, L., & McLaughlin, M. W. (1995). Policies that support professional development in an era of reform. *Phi Delta Kappan, 76*(8), 597-604.

Dasho, S., & Kendzior, S. (1995, April). *Toward a caring community of learning for teachers: Staff development to support the Child Development Project.* Symposium conducted at the meeting of the American Educational Research Association, San Francisco. Oakland, CA: Developmental Studies Center.

Elmore, R. F., with Burney, D. (1996). *Staff development and instructional improvement in Community District 2, New York City.* Paper prepared for the National Commission on Teaching and America's Future.

Elmore, R. F., & McLaughlin, M. (1988). *Steady work: Policy, practice, and reform in American education.* Santa Monica, CA: RAND.

Erikson, E. (1963). *Childhood and society.* New York: Macmillan.

Fessler, R., & Christensen, J. (1992, April). *Teacher career cycle model: A framework for viewing teacher growth needs.* Paper presented at the Annual Meeting of the American Research Association, Montreal, Quebec.

Fullan, M. (1991). *The new meaning of change.* New York: Teachers College Press.

Guskey, T. (1986, May). Staff development and the process of teacher change. *Educational Researcher,* pp. 5-12.

Huberman, M. (1995). Professional careers and professional development: Some intersections. In T. Guskey & M. Huberman (Eds.), *Professional development in education: New paradigms and practices.* New York: Teachers College Press.

Levinson, D. (1978). *The seasons of a man's life.* New York: Knopf.

Lieberman, A. (1995a). Practices that support teacher development: Transforming conceptions of professional learning. *Phi Delta Kappan, 76*(8), 591-596.

Lieberman, A. (1995b). *The work of restructuring the schools: Building from the ground up.* New York: Teachers College Press.

Lieberman, A., & Grolnick, M. (1996). Networks and the reform of American education. *Teachers College Record, 98*(1), 7-45.

Lieberman, A., & McLaughlin, M. W. (1992). Networks for educational change: Powerful and problematic. *Phi Delta Kappan, 73*(9), 673-677.

Lieberman, A., & Miller, L. (1990, June). Restructuring schools: What matters and what works. *Phi Delta Kappan, 71*(10), 759-764.

Lieberman, A., & Miller, L. (Eds.). (1991). *Staff development for education in the 90's: New demands, new realities, new perspectives.* New York: Teachers College Press.

Little, J. W. (1993). Teachers' professional development in a climate of educational reform. *Educational Evaluation and Policy Analysis, 15*(2), 129-151.

Little, J. W. (1996, January). *Organizing schools for teacher learning.* Paper presented at the Area Conference on Teacher Development and School Reform, Washington, DC.

Little, J. W., Gerritz, W. H., Stern, D. S., Guthrie, J. W., Kirst, M. W., & Marsh, D. D. (1987). *Staff development in California: Public and personal investment, program patterns, and policy choices.* San Francisco: Far West Laboratory for Educational Research and Development.

Little, J. W., & McLaughlin, M. W. (1991). *Urban mathematics collaboratives: As the teachers tell it.* Stanford, CA: Stanford University, Center for Research on the Context of Secondary School Teaching.

Lord, B. (1991, April). *Subject-area collaboratives, teacher professionalism, and staff development.* Paper presented at the annual meeting of the American Educational Research Association, Chicago.

Loucks-Horsley, S., & Stiegelbauer, S. (1991). Using knowledge of change to guide staff development. In A. Lieberman & L. Miller (Eds.), *Staff development for education in the 90's: New demands, new realities, new perspectives.* New York: Teachers College Press.

McLaughlin, M. W. (1998). Listening and learning from the field: Tales of policy implementation and situated practice. In A. Lieberman (Ed.), *The international handbook of educational change: Vol. 1. The roots of educational change* (pp. 70-84). Dordrecht, The Netherlands: Kluwer.

McLaughlin, M. W., & Talbert, J. (1993). *Contexts that matter for teaching and learning.* Stanford, CA: Center for Research on the Context of Secondary School Teaching, Stanford University.

Newmann, F., & Wehlage, G. (1995). *Successful school restructuring: A report to the public and educators.* Madison: Center on Organization and Restructuring of Schools, Wisconsin Center for Education Research, University of Wisconsin.

Senge, P. (1990). *The fifth discipline: The art and practice of the learning organization.* New York: Currency Books.

Showers, B., Joyce, B., & Bennett, B. (1987). Synthesis of research on staff development: A framework for future study and a state-of-the art analysis. *Educational Leadership, 45*(3), 77-87.

Sparks, D., & Loucks-Horsley, S. (1990). Models of staff development. In W. R. Houston, M. Haberman, & J. Skula (Eds.), *Handbook of research on teacher education* (pp. 234-250). New York: Macmillan.

CHAPTER 8

Designing and Implementing School-Based Professional Development

Linda Valli
Willis D. Hawley
University of Maryland

Many teachers approach staff development "opportunities" with re-luctance—or dread. Their experience has been with the sit-and-get, one-size-fits-all, quick-fix model—a model that has failed to respect teachers' knowledge, contribute to school improvement, or advance student learning. In Michael Fullan's judgment, these workshops and conferences have been a terrible waste because they have not led to significant changes in practice. Fortunately, a new model of professional development that recognizes schools as complex organizations, learning as an interactive process, and teachers as competent learners is gradually taking hold.

Our review of recent research, policy documents, and school change processes indicates that there is a growing consensus about nine basic principles that can serve as the foundation for new models of professional development. We call these nine principles the "essentials" of effective professional development. They support Lieberman and Miller's arguments in Chapter 7 that (a) professional development and school improvement

AUTHORS' NOTE: This chapter revises and updates conclusions we reported and documented in Willis D. Hawley and Linda Valli, "The Essentials of Effective Professional Development: A new consensus," in L. Darling-Hammond and G. Sykes (Eds.), *The Heart of the Matter: Teaching Is the Learning Profession*. San Francisco: Jossey-Bass, 1999, pp. 127-150. Much of this work was funded by the Office of Educational Research and Development, U.S. Department of Education.

must be closely linked, and (b) this linkage is facilitated by attending to teachers' professional concerns, the culture and organization of the school, and external support networks. In this chapter, we explain these principles as well as the forces that account for the consensus that supports them. In the process, we provide examples of how this new, more rewarding and effective model of professional development can be implemented.

Design Principles

The design principles we have constructed from research syntheses and recent calls for action—such as those of the American Federation of Teachers, the National Education Association, the National Governor's Association, the National Institute for Science Education, the National Staff Development Council, and the U.S. Department of Education—focus attention on improving student learning through the improvement of teacher learning. Professional development is more likely to result in substantive and lasting changes in the knowledge, skills, and behaviors of educators that enhance student learning when it includes these characteristics:

1. *The content of professional development (PD) focuses on what students are to learn and how to address the different problems students may have in learning that material.* The content of professional development is critically important to its effectiveness. Although the focus will vary with the goals of the school or district, professional development should deal directly with what students are expected to learn and the instructional strategies best suited to teach that content. Professional development should be aligned closely with the specific content students are expected to learn.

Providing teachers with general information about an instructional procedure (e.g., how to use cooperative-learning techniques) or enrichment courses on subject material (e.g., new developments in biology) usually does not result in improved teaching. Instead, professional development should focus on the specific content that students are expected to learn, problems students might confront in learning the content, and instructional strategies that address anticipated problems or issues. Although teachers must know substantially more about a subject than their students, higher-level content knowledge should be tied to the particular lessons students are to learn if teachers are to be expected to use this knowledge to enhance student learning. Teachers also need to learn how to adapt instructional strategies to variations in student needs and learning contexts. Teaching teachers that there is only one way to teach a lesson can be counterproductive.

2. Professional development should be driven by analyses of the differences between (a) goals and standards for student learning, and (b) student performance. Analyses of the differences between goals and standards for student learning and student performance will define what educators need to learn, make professional development student centered, and increase public confidence in the use of resources for professional development. Educators can then use these analyses to explore the usefulness of alternative strategies for student learning and school improvement, paying close attention to the gains made by diverse types of learners.

The importance of this student-centered focus seems self-evident, but it has not been standard practice. Too often, new teaching strategies, curricular redesign, or organizational restructuring, pursued as goals in and of themselves, have diverted attention from the school's central goal. Moreover, school-level educators too often have been given little help in developing analytic capacity for continual school improvement and discouraged from engaging in systematic analysis by bureaucratic structures. A 1996 study of a change effort in the Chicago public schools, for example, found diminished capacity in schools because the central school office assumed the functions of identifying problems, creating responsive programs, and evaluating their effectiveness (Bryk, Rollow, & Pinnell, 1996). School-based educators will be more motivated to learn if they themselves identify the problem, dilemma, or need on the basis of their analysis of how well students are learning.

3. Professional development should involve teachers in the identification of what they need to learn and, when possible, in the development of the learning opportunity or the process to be used. Engagement in the process increases educators' motivation and commitment to learn, encourages them to take instructional risks and to assume new roles, and increases the likelihood that what is learned will be meaningful and relevant to particular contexts and problems. If teachers are denied input to their own professional development, they are likely to become cynical and detached from school improvement efforts.

There are so many possibilities for learning so many things that school leaders must keep attention focused on what teachers really need to learn to close the gap between school goals and school performance. For example, teachers are not likely to identify a need for subject matter knowledge or pedagogical content knowledge. Professional credibility and teaching effectiveness depend on teachers "knowing" the material they teach students. Yet understandings of mathematics, science, history, and the arts—and how to teach those subjects—have changed radically in recent years. School leaders must create organizational cultures in which everyone feels good about needing to learn. They must also protect teachers from unnecessary and unproductive involvement, unreasonable expectations, and burnout.

  4. Professional development should be primarily school based and integral to school operations. School-based professional development does not mean denying teachers access to out-of-school learning experiences through professional associations or networks, graduate study, or teacher centers. But the most powerful opportunities to learn are often connected with the recognition of and solution to authentic and immediate problems. Motivation to learn and to engage in school change efforts also increases when these efforts are linked to improving and assessing daily practice. The optimal workplace is one in which learning arises from and feeds back into work experience, where learning is considered to be part of work.

  This type of "job-embedded" learning not only links learning to problems, it allows teachers to see new strategies modeled, practice them, engage in peer coaching, acclimate students to new ways of learning, use new teaching and learning strategies on a regular and appropriate basis, and see the effects of newly learned behaviors. School systems simply must build teacher learning time into the school day. Teachers need a significant amount of instruction, with follow-up days of technical assistance, to develop new pedagogical skills. Such time can be built into the school day through flexible scheduling; by extending the school year; by repurposing meetings; and through other creative strategies, such as "banking" time.

  5. Professional development should provide learning opportunities that relate to individual needs but are, for the most part, organized around collaborative problem solving. Even though collaborative cultures facilitate school improvement and teacher learning, as currently structured, most schools still isolate teachers from one another. There is little opportunity for purposeful social interaction. Teachers are too often asked to change their instruction in isolation and without support. Collaborative problem-solving activities can vary from interdisciplinary teaming to curriculum development and critique to collaborative action research to study groups. In each case, educators working together to address issues of common concern facilitate the identification of both causes of and potential solutions to problems.

When done skillfully, collaborative problem-solving leads to the clarification of learning needs and the sharing of knowledge and expertise. It breaks down teacher isolation, empowers teachers, creates an environment of professional respect, and develops a shared language and understanding of good practice. School cultures that promote a genuine sense of collective purpose and provide support systems motivate teacher engagement in continuous learning.

6. *Professional development should be continuous and ongoing, involving follow-up and support for further learning—including support from sources external to the school that can provide necessary resources and an outside perspective.* As what is learned from professional development is implemented, learners often discover what they need to be effective. If that need for learning, resources, and support is not met, increased professional competence and student achievement are unlikely to be experienced and the motivation to engage in additional professional development will be affected. Although most professional development should be school based, educators also need to enrich this learning with new ideas and knowledge gained from sources beyond the school. Innovation is constrained if informed only by those who share similar ideas and experiences.

Pedagogical change also requires time to learn new things well and to establish trust and shared meanings with those inside and outside the school organization. It is not uncommon to find that it takes 3 to 5 years to bring about significant change in educational practice. Ongoing support is especially critical in the first 2 years of implementation. The public expects, however, to see quick changes in schools and concrete evidence of improvements in student achievement.

7. *Professional development should incorporate evaluation of multiple sources of information on (a) outcomes for students, and (b) processes that are involved in implementing the lessons learned through professional development.* Teachers' knowledge and experience as well as research studies and outside consultants should be valued sources of information. The evaluation can be done by school-based educators, outside evaluators, or (and probably best) a joint team. It should be nonthreatening and conducted throughout various stages of implementation, allow sufficient time for change to occur, assess change in teaching before assessing change in student learning, and help teachers think more carefully about their classroom practice. Knowing the extent to which professional development has

influenced student achievement contributes to the design of and incentives for further professional learning.

8. Professional development should provide opportunities to engage in developing a theoretical understanding of the knowledge and skills to be learned. Results of research, in comprehensible forms, need to be made accessible to teachers, who often cite lack of understanding and limited access as reasons why they do not put theory into practice. Teacher thinking and classroom behavior are deeply influenced by teachers' knowledge and beliefs. Thus an important component of professional development needs to be the expansion and elaboration of teachers' professional knowledge base. Broadly speaking, this would include general pedagogical knowledge, subject matter knowledge, and pedagogical content knowledge, which address such areas as classroom management, conceptions of teaching a subject, and students' understandings and potential misunderstandings of subject matter.

But new knowledge in itself does not bring about change. Professional development must engage teachers' beliefs, experiences, and habits. Providing opportunities for teachers to learn new practices requires an understanding of how teachers gain perspective on their own beliefs and actions when confronted with new theories and practices. Effective professional development may require that teachers reconsider fundamental beliefs. Teachers must experience different types of learning themselves, spend time adapting their instruction, and see positive results in their students. But since beliefs filter knowledge and guide behavior, significant transformations of teaching practice are unlikely to occur if related beliefs and theories about teaching and learning do not change.

9. Professional development should be integrated with a comprehensive change process that deals with impediments to and facilitators of student learning. Teachers are asked too often to learn things they cannot act on because there is no organizational commitment to continuous experimentation and improvement. Professional development must be part of a systemic change effort that includes district, school, and individual components, as well as the intervention of external facilitators and technical advisors. Otherwise, professional development has little probability of changing school norms and teaching practice. This collective approach to teacher learning means that professional development activities are not left primarily to an individual incentive system. Rather, they are part of the structure, culture, and reward system of the workplace.

Basis for Consensus

As suggested earlier, the new consensus about these basic principles has come about, in part, from teachers' dissatisfaction with years of staff development that is disconnected from the realities of their daily experience. In addition to dissatisfaction with this weak model of staff development, at least three other influences have converged to create the conditions for this new consensus:

- The link between professional development and school improvement
- Higher standards for students
- Research on learning

Professional Development and School Improvement

One factor that has brought about consensus on these basic principles of professional development is our heightened understanding of the link between professional development and school improvement. One of the most persistent findings from research on school improvement is the close relation between professional development and school improvement efforts. The two processes are so tightly woven that their effects are almost impossible to disentangle. This observation takes on critical importance in light of the finding that teacher quality, skill, and opportunities to learn might well be the most important factors in student learning.

Higher Standards for Students

A second influence on the new consensus about effective professional development is the increased demand for higher student standards. As long as school improvement was defined as increasing the level and amount of facts and simple skills students must learn, the job of teaching was seen as a fairly simple task of transmitting what teachers know and texts explain. This view of "teaching as telling" is reasonable when one does not expect all students to achieve at relatively high levels. Traditional conceptions of teaching and learning assign the job of learning to students. This means that teachers can be seen largely as organizers of student activity and thus in need of limited opportunities to improve their teaching. If teaching is believed to involve few pedagogical skills and is intuitively sensible, it can be learned in teacher preparation programs and by experience; there would be little need for significant ongoing professional development.

The character of the knowledge and skills that students must have to participate in a culturally diverse democracy and an information-based economy is changing rapidly and coming to be defined in terms of criteria we have until now expected only some students to meet. As we learn more about how students learn, and as we insist that students master more complex knowledge and develop greater capabilities for problem solving, "teaching by telling" is being replaced by "teaching for understanding." In other words, teaching matters more when we set our goals for learning higher. If we expect all students to attain new and more challenging learning goals, goals that emphasize sustained and rigorous inquiry, teachers must also have opportunities to learn new material, new ways of thinking and teaching, better ways of connecting with an increasingly diverse range of students, and ways to construct and use appropriate curriculum and assessments.

Research on Learning

A third influence on this new consensus is research on cognitive development that has significantly altered fundamental understandings of how and why people learn. Although those who do research on cognition differ on many issues, there are a number of core beliefs related to how people learn about which most researchers appear to agree. Alexander and Murphy (1998) have reviewed the relevant research and identified five "learner-centered principles" that summarize the findings of many studies:

Knowledge Base Principle. A person's existing knowledge serves as a foundation of future learning by guiding the organization and representation of new ideas, by serving as a basis of association with new information, and by filtering new experience. People engage new knowledge and skills through the lens of past experience. Teachers bring to their work a host of prior beliefs, ideas, and values about teaching, assessment, subject matter knowledge, and students. These prior beliefs influence their approach to staff development, what they learn from it, and how they change their classroom practice. Thus creating effective professional development opportunities requires an understanding of how teachers make connections between what they know and how they learn.

Strategic Processing Principle. Reflecting on and regulating one's own thoughts and actions is essential to learning. Even more than children, adults have a deep need to be self-directed learners. They must be meaningfully engaged in studying, creating, and evaluating their professional work. Professional development strategies must foster self-monitoring skills so teachers can develop and assess expertise in new areas. To be self-monitoring, teachers must acquire inquiry skills of data collection, analysis, interpretation, evaluation, and reflection.

Development Principle. Although everyone's experiences are unique, learning does proceed through common stages of development that are influenced by both inherited and experiential or environmental factors. As Lieberman and Miller explained in their review of the literature on career development in this volume, teachers pass through both life and professional stages. To maximize the impact of professional development, these stages should be taken into account. Study teams, for example, should include teachers at different stages of their careers. Through heterogeneous pairing, activities such as peer coaching can be more effectively employed than is possible when peers are "well matched."

Motivation Principle. Intrinsic motivation, attributions for learning, personal goals, and the motivational characteristics of learning tasks strongly influence the learning process. Learning opportunities for teachers must attend to these social and psychological factors since they affect teachers' perceptions about the desirability of change. Proposals for change must be consistent with teachers' learning goals and interests. If they are not, evidence must be developed to persuade teachers that the changes will bring about better conditions for teaching and learning.

Context Principle. Learning is both a socially shared and an individually constructed enterprise. In addition to believing that a particular change is desirable, teachers must also be convinced that it is possible. They must believe that they have—or will have—the skill and resources necessary to effect change. Those who guide professional development experiences must understand classroom contexts and must be able to frame their information in ways that are not only comprehensible but feasible for teachers. Harm is done through professional development promises that cannot be delivered—teachers' hopes are raised, then shattered; and they become suspicious of, then resistant to, any innovation.

These learning principles explain why most traditional professional development activities are relatively ineffective. They simply do not build on prior knowledge; actively involve teachers in the learning process; acknowledge factors that inspire teachers to learn; attend to individual stages of development; or embed learning in authentic, collaborative contexts. If these principles of learning shaped the opportunities to learn that are available to educators, professional development would look quite different from the way it does now.

Conclusion

The essential characteristic of effective professional development is that it involves continuous teacher and administrator learning in the context of collaborative problem solving. When professional development is thought of as a discreet program or a series of formal scheduled events or is otherwise disconnected from authentic problem solving, it is unlikely to have much influence on teacher or student learning. This means that schools need to be structured in ways that provide educators with opportunities to learn as they collectively address the challenges posed by the inevitable gap between high standards and actual student performance.

References and Resources

Alexander, P. A., & Murphy, P. K. (1998). The research base for APA's learner-centered psychological principles. In N. L. Lambert & B. L. McCombs (Eds.), *Issues in school reform: A sampler of psychological perspectives on learner-centered schools* (pp. 25-60). Washington, DC: American Psychological Association.

Bransford, J., Brown, A., & Cocking, R. (Eds.). (1999). *How people learn: Brain, mind, experience and school.* Washington, DC: National Academy Press.

Bryk, A. S., Rollow, S. G., & Pinnell, G. S. (1996). Urban school development: Literacy as a lever for change. *Educational Policy, 10*(2), 172-201.

Corcoran, T. C. (1995). *Helping teachers teach well: Transforming professional development.* New Brunswick, NJ: Consortium for Policy Research in Education, Rutgers University.

Darling-Hammond, L. S., & Sykes, G. (Eds.). (1998). *The heart of the matter: Teaching as a learning profession.* San Francisco: Jossey-Bass.

Fullan, M. (1991). *The new meaning of educational change.* New York: Teachers College Press.

Guskey, T. R., & Huberman, M. (Eds.). (1995). *Professional development in education: New paradigms and practices* (pp. 35-66). New York: Teachers College Press.

Joyce, B., & Showers, B. (1995). *Student achievement through staff development: Fundamentals of school renewal* (2nd ed.). White Plains, NY: Longman.

National Commission on Teaching and America's Future. (1996). *What matters most: Teaching for America's future.* New York: Author.

National Staff Development Council. (1994). *Standards for staff development.* Oxford, OH: Author.

Newmann, F. M., & Wehlage, G. G. (1995). *Successful school restructuring: A report to the public and educators.* Madison: Center on Organization and Restructuring of Schools, Wisconsin Center for Education Research, University of Wisconsin–Madison.

U.S. Department of Education. (1995). *Building bridges: The mission and principles of professional development.* Washington, DC: Author.

CHAPTER 9

Organizational Conditions to Support Teaching and Learning

Kenneth Leithwood

Ontario Institute for Studies in Education
University of Toronto

In a context of declining resources, escalating expectations for student learning, and turbulent environments, schools need to be "designed" so that changing is considered an ordinary activity rather than an extraordinary event. At the heart of any organization's capacity for such continuous improvement is the individual and collective learning of its members (e.g., Peterson, McCarthey, & Elmore, 1996). For example, improving the school's instructional services, and thereby improving students' learning, requires considerable learning on the part of teachers, as well as those providing administrative and other forms of support for teachers.

Appreciation of the importance of such collective professional learning has given rise to a venerable body of research on "organizational learning" processes in nonschool organizations (for a comprehensive review of this literature, see Cousins, 1996) and a quite recent literature about such processes in schools (Leithwood, 2000; Leithwood & Louis, 1999). Describing seven sets of conditions that enhance the likelihood of organizational learning in schools is the purpose of this chapter. These conditions are related to schools' mission and goals, culture, structure and organization, information collection and decision-making processes, policies and procedures, school-community partnerships, and leadership.

Mission and Goals

The official source of a school's purpose is often found in a written "mission" statement. Such statements describe the school's explicit conception of what it would like to accomplish. An implicit source of direction is to be found in the norms, values, beliefs, and assumptions shared by members of the organization—the organization's culture. Depending on the form and content of the culture, these two sources of direction—mission and culture—may be mutually supportive, unrelated, or actually in conflict (Bolman & Deal, 1991).

A school's explicit mission and goals are powerful determinants of individual and collective professional learning when they are used by members of the school to help them understand and evaluate information coming to them from outside sources or as feedback from actions taken within the school. Serving as "perceptual screens," the mission and goals potentially help people decide what to attend to from the full array of demands, expectations, and information with which they come into contact.

For a school's mission and goals to serve as a stimulus for action, school staff and other stakeholders need to be aware of them. Furthermore, the mission and goals must be clear and personally meaningful to the members; this is most likely to be the case when the mission and goals are an expression of fundamental values held by members of the school and the people served by the school. When these conditions are met, the mission and goals serve as criteria for decision making at every level.

Such active use of the school's mission and goals develops when they are created with the extensive involvement of staff, through a process that encourages sustained and serious discussion, and when the initial outcome of that discussion is subject to continuous review and refinement (Wallace, 1996; Wilson & Corcoran, 1988).

Culture

A school's organizational culture is "a system of ordinary, taken-for-granted meanings and symbols with both implicit and explicit content [i.e., norms, values, beliefs, assumptions] that is, deliberately and non-deliberately, learned and shared among members" (Erickson, 1987, p. 12). There are three dimensions to a school's culture: its *form, content,* and *strength.*

With respect to *form,* a school's culture may vary from one that largely supports isolated, individual work and problem solving to one that is based on collaboration in its various forms, from collaboration among subgroups in the organization ("balkanized") to whole staff collaboration (Hargreaves & Macmillan, 1991). Evidence suggests a strong link between highly collaborative school cultures and schools' effectiveness (Fieman-Nemser & Floden, 1986; Little, 1982). Authentic collaboration among teachers, about the improvement of teaching and learning, for example, provides opportunities for the dissemination of hard-won technical knowledge from one teacher to another. It also provides occasions for joint problem solving around individual teacher dilemmas as well as tasks shared by teachers, such as curriculum development tasks.

The specific nature of a school staff's shared norms, values, beliefs, and assumptions defines the *content* of a school's culture. Staff in especially productive schools typically hold norms of continuous improvement and professional growth as well as norms of mutual respect. These staff value the welfare and learning of their students first and foremost. As well, they value the participation of all the school's stakeholders in decision making and believe that all of their students can learn and that they are responsible for ensuring that such learning occurs (Mortimore, Sammons, Stoll, Lewis, & Ecob, 1988; Rosenholtz, 1989).

The extent to which norms, values, beliefs, and assumptions are shared among staff defines the strength of a school's culture. Strong cultures are especially useful in the day-to-day conduct of the school's business because the hectic and fast-paced nature of the enterprise provides little opportunity for collegial deliberation (Hargreaves & Macmillan, 1991). Excessive consensus among staff can be self-sealing, however, cutting off the inclination to award ideas for change the attention they may deserve (Firestone & Louis, 1999). Indeed, learning what is needed for organizational improvement demands openness to new ideas from diverse sources, along with norms of risk taking and experimentation and beliefs about the importance of learning from small failures (Sitkin, 1992; Watkins & Marsick, 1993).

Evidence concerning how less productive school cultures can be changed is modest, but recommends several strategies: using such bureaucratic strategies as the hiring of new staff to support cultural norms; persistently communicating the values considered to be important to the culture; providing symbolic support, for example, through ceremonies, for the values and beliefs considered important to the school; and providing staff development activities that empower staff to act in ways valued by the school (Deal & Peterson, 1990; Leithwood & Jantzi, 1990).

Structure and Organization

An organization's structure is "an outline of the desired patterns of activities, expectations and exchanges" (Bolman & Deal, 1991, p. 46) among members of the organization and the people they serve. Schools, like many other types of organizations, are attempting to become more adaptive and flexible. One way of doing this is by moving from relatively hierarchical, centralized structures that function well in predictable environments to more organic, decentralized, and fluid structures that acknowledge the turbulent and unpredictable context in which schools now find themselves (Banner & Gagne, 1995; Morgan, 1986). Decentralized school structures potentially encourage learning and reflective action-taking by spreading, to multiple members of the school, the demands for thinking about new information. This reduces the number of things individuals have to think about at one time, making it easier for them to assimilate those new patterns of practice.

Evidence is compelling that teachers' participation in school decisions has positive effects on their work (e.g., Conley, 1993). Furthermore, these effects can be achieved without implementing the various forms of site-based management so popular across the country at present. Site-based management has proven to be very difficult to implement adequately (Leithwood & Menzies, 1998a; Malen & Ogawa, 1988) and has yet to demonstrate many of the consequences for which it is advocated (Leithwood & Menzies, 1998b; Murphy & Beck, 1995).

In sum, collective and individual professional learning in schools is most likely to be stimulated by school structures that encourage collective problem solving, allocate responsibility and accountability for decision making to those most directly affected by decisions, avoid wasting people's time on decisions that do not effect them and about which they have no special knowledge, and provide those involved with ready access to the information they require for their decision making.

Information-Collection and Decision-Making Processes

My answers reflect a lack of knowledge, understanding and guidance of "proposed" curricula of the states reform policy. Also, there is a strongly felt lack of communication between staff and administration about goals, decision-making-sharing processes, implementation of changes.[1]

The other day, I asked for feedback from the staff on how it [a peer tutoring program] was going and what their perception of it was. We have 40 people on staff and I got feedback from 18 or 19. I fed back to them the information I got and then we engaged in an open dialogue on how things could be improved. . . .

The school decided last year to institute an S.S.R. [silent reading program] to run each morning. It was not just a hasty decision made by a small group of people or just by the administration and then imposed. It took months and months of a committee of interested people working on it. There was a lot of input like surveys; questions; the kids were surveyed. It was almost too much; it was almost too slow. Eventually, when it finally started last fall, nobody could say that their voice had not been heard. The thing was examined thoroughly and done very well.

"Garbage in, garbage out" is an old adage sometimes used in the context of statistical data analysis. No amount of sophistication in statistical analysis will compensate for information collected poorly in the first place. Something similar is true of organizational learning in schools. The quality of that learning depends significantly on the amount and quality of information available to members of the organization to assist in their learning (McGrath, 1986); it also depends on the methods used for processing that information (Gersick & Davis-Sacks, 1991; Goodman and Associates, 1986).

The quotations opening this section illustrate several approaches a school might take to information collection (or provision) and decision making. The first teacher's response indicates that apparently little or no information was made available to the teacher by the school. This resulted in feelings of confusion and hostility on the part of the teacher and no learning likely to improve the teacher's practices. Furthermore, the teacher's remarks suggest little or no participation in decision making about how to respond to the state's initiative. The second and third quotations are in stark contrast to the first, indicating highly participative forms of decision making informed by considerable amounts of carefully accumulated data. The second teacher describes how this can be done quite nimbly; the process described by the third teacher is clearly more protracted, perhaps even ponderous in her view, but likely useful in the long term nonetheless. Organizational learning is a likely outcome of circumstances illustrated by the second and third quotations. Obviously, having access to relevant information expands decision alternatives and provides a firmer basis for choosing between those alternatives.

The participation of all relevant stakeholders assumes that many heads are capable of better sense making than is one, an assumption for which Simon (1996) has provided compelling theoretical justification. Nonetheless, teams or groups often do not live up this potential. Indeed Janis (1982) coined the term "groupthink" to describe the unproductive nature of much group work. Fostering productive problem solving in groups depends on creating a set of conditions, including the encouragement of divergent views, open expression of ideas, awareness of the knowledge and other limits of the group, recognition of the unique contributions each member of the group is capable of making, and willingness by the group to engage in the discussion of collective doubts (Hackman, 1991; Neck & Manz, 1994). The creation of these conditions usually depends on team leadership and a supportive culture of the sort described above.

Policies and Procedures

Several of [the state's initiatives] are very good and are ideal, but then so was communism. Making it work in practice and having it be a beautiful ideal are two different things.

District-level initiative has already died. Committee formation [is] ignored by secondary teachers; teachers want a very specific instruction outline, "What do you want me to teach, with what students and how?"; [the state] guidelines are either vague or impossible.

What I teach in the classroom is driven by curriculum. We can delete or add as we see fit but certainly the curriculum is the guide. I do personal professional development by going to workshops, science workshops or conferences. But the school-based pro-D is not curriculum oriented.

The principal and the vice principal were very careful when they did their hiring to select people with the same sort of philosophies, the same sort of ideas, and they had us all get together last June, they had us get together in April, May, picking materials, looking at our different resources, planning what we would like in our classrooms; so they pulled us together way before the full year even started.

These comments by teachers illustrate a variety of responses to policy (the first two), expectations for policy (the second and third), and the ways policies and procedures can be used productively as instruments to support school improvement efforts (the last). The first quotation exemplifies a view of *policy as sometimes unworkable philosophy*. From this view, it is possible, at the same time, to agree with a philosophy (or policy) and to continue with practices not supported by the philosophy. Schön (1987) describes this apparent paradox as a gap between espoused theory and theory-in-use. Senge (1990) argues that until the gap is overcome, significant learning is unlikely to occur. This is so because such a gap probably indicates only surface understanding of the espoused theory; it is also probably symptomatic of a much more deeply understood but unrecognized theory actually guiding a teacher's practices. Individual and collective staff learning is helped when people are encouraged to discover their theories-in-use and compare those theories with theories espoused by policy. As a consequence, the gap between the two is likely to be reduced and policies can become real guides to action.

The second quotation illustrates two matters of importance in fostering individual and collective professional learning. First, policies and procedures serve symbolic as well as more instrumental purposes: The death of district-level "initiatives" (i.e., procedures) signifies to this teacher lack of commitment by the district to the implementation of the state's initiatives. As a consequence, in this teacher's view, commitment to the effort on the part of his or her colleagues has also dissipated. District policies and procedures indicate to staff indirectly and symbolically, as well as directly, what learning is of most worth to the district. Improvements to teaching and learning are fostered by the maintenance of a relatively consistent, meaningful policy focus at school, district, and state levels. Because such consistency across levels of the school system is rare, schools need to be proactive in developing their own school improvement plans and using these plans as defense against external incoherence.

The second quotation also illustrates a view of *policy as specifications for action*. This teacher complains of vagueness, of no specifications of when, who, or how. It is a complaint founded on assumptions about the role of teacher as technician, about the classroom as a predictable environment for instruction, about solutions to problems of improvement as already discovered but not yet disseminated (Fullan, 1993). These assumptions are untenable in a school that values continuous progress because they suggest that learning is somebody else's responsibility. Schools that value continuous progress encourage their members to give up such assumptions and pursue, instead, the goal of personal mastery (Senge, 1990). They do this in part by creating as few policies as possible, policies that do not restrict people from using their own good judgment (Morgan, 1986), and by ensuring coherence between policies and organizational mission (Fuhrman, 1993).

The last two quotations illustrate the potential of school-level policies and procedures either to serve the functions of school improvement quite directly or to be, at best, tangential to them. The final quotation illustrates direct, instrumental use of policy for improvement purposes, whereas the third quotation illustrates how school-based professional development policies can miss the opportunity of being more directly useful.

School-Community Partnerships

Closer and more extensive relationships between districts, schools, and their communities is a central pillar of many current educational restructuring initiatives (e.g., Darling-Hammond, 1993). These relationships take many forms, for example, local governing councils for schools in Great Britain that have opted out of their local educational authorities (Walford, 1993), parent-dominated decision bodies for local schools in Chicago and parts of Australia (Caldwell & Hayward, 1998), and various forms of parent involvement directly in student work at home and in the classroom (Lareau, 1989). Reasons for such relationships between schools and their local communities include helping some parents improve their parenting skills and foster conditions in the home that support learning, providing parents with knowledge of educational techniques to assist children learning at home, and providing access to and coordinating community and support services for children and families (Leithwood & Joong, 1993). Closer school-community relationships are also intended to promote clear two-way communication between the school and the family regarding school programs and student progress; involve parents in instructional support roles at school; support parents as decision makers and develop their leadership in governance, advisory, and advocacy roles; and use community resources and opportunities to strengthen the school program.

Community relationships may be developed in ways that foster organizational learning. Teachers often express apprehension about greater parent participation in school (Lareau, 1989), yet parents are a rich source of information about the instructional needs of their students, sometimes able to predict school conditions that foster student learning better than teachers (Snydor & Ebmeier, 1992). Parents also bring fresh perspectives to the school about priorities for education and more specific causes of students' responses to instruction. When parents value the instruction being received by their children, they also become the most powerful allies that teachers can have.

Leadership

School leadership is one of the most significant factors influencing the success of school improvement efforts (Hallinger & Heck, 1996; Leithwood, Jantzi, & Steinbach, 1999). But the context for leadership is a powerful determinant of the forms of leadership that will be useful. The contextually determined nature of leadership discourages efforts to define, in general, the specific behaviors of effective leaders. Rather, it encourages the view that leadership is situational and context dependent (Duke, 1987; Shamir & Howell, 1999). When staff members experience lack of leadership, the problem may be one of fit. For example, Susan brings to her new job boundless energy, ambitious visions, and a strong commitment to school reform. But Susan succeeds Tony, who had the same qualities and was successful in helping staff initiate a large bundle of changes in the school during the 3 years of his tenure. The staff are in the midst of refining their knowledge, "working out the kinks" in these changes, and recovering from the ubiquitous "implementation dip" (Fullan, 1991). The support they need, at this point, is easily accessible technical assistance (Louis & Miles, 1992) and a stable school environment with limited distractions from their efforts to consolidate the changes they have made. They also need help in assessing whether the changes they have made are paying off as anticipated. From Susan's perspective, this is sort of dull work and not at all taking advantage of her strengths.

As a minimum, then, efforts to describe school leadership must acknowledge the importance of situation and context; this means allowing for variation in leadership style and behavior. It is possible to do this and still endorse a particular model of leadership when the model fits the broad challenges being experienced by many reforming and restructuring schools and when considerable variation in behavior in the model is possible. Evidence suggests that a transformational model of leadership is productive in restructuring schools (Leithwood, 1994).

Roberts's (1985) synopsis of transformational leadership sounds a lot like what Susan is keen to offer:

> This type of leadership offers a vision of what could be and gives a sense of purpose and meaning to those who would share that vision. It builds

commitment, enthusiasm, and excitement. It creates a hope in the future and a belief that the world is knowable, understandable, and manageable. The collective action that transforming leadership generates empowers those who participate in the process. There is hope, there is optimism, there is energy. In essence, transforming leadership is a leadership that facilitates the redefinition of a people's mission and vision, a renewal of their commitment, and the restructuring of their systems for goal accomplishment. (p. 1024)

But research concerning the meaning of transformational leadership in practice suggests that it is multidimensional (e.g., Podsakoff, MacKenzie, Moorman, & Fetter, 1990). It is concerned, as is Susan, with developing a vision, fostering acceptance of group goals, and providing intellectual stimulation. But it is also concerned with providing support to individual staff members as they grapple with changing their practices; it is about monitoring high performance expectations in the face of learning new behaviors; and it also includes setting an example for staff to follow that is consistent with the values espoused by the district or school. Each of these dimensions of transformational leadership can be carried out through a variety of quite different, specific behaviors.

Conclusion

It is tempting to argue that efforts to improve teaching and learning are most effective when they focus directly on the relationships between teachers and students, that talented teachers will do good work in any kind of school organization. This argument fails to account for the evidence suggesting that even the most well meaning and enthusiastic teachers are unable to sustain serious changes in their practices in the context of school organizations that are (usually inadvertently) hostile to those changes (Louis & Miles, 1992; Randi & Corno, 1997). The institutionalization of significant change requires its advocates to become organizational "designers."

Note

1. The quotations from teachers in this chapter are from a research study, the results of which are reported in Leithwood, Jantzi, and Steinbach (1995).

References and Resources

Banner, D. K., & Gagne, T. E. (1995). *Designing effective organizations: Traditional and transformational views.* Thousand Oaks, CA: Sage.

Bolman, L. G., & Deal, T. E. (1991). *Reframing organizations.* San Francisco: Jossey-Bass.

Caldwell, B. J., & Hayward, D. (1998). *The future of schools: Lessons from the reform of public education.* London: Falmer.

Conley, D. T. (1993). *Roadmap to restructuring.* Eugene: University of Oregon. (ERIC Clearinghouse on Educational Management No. EA024472)

Cousins, J. B. (1996). Understanding organizational learning for educational leadership and school reform. In K. Leithwood, J. Chapman, & D. Corson (Eds.), *International handbook of educational leadership and administration* (pp. 589-652). Dordrecht, The Netherlands: Kluwer.

Darling-Hammond, L. (1993). Reframing the school reform agenda. *Phi Delta Kappan 75*(10), pp. 753-761.

Deal, T., & Peterson, K. (1990). *The principal's role in shaping school culture.* Washington, DC: U.S. Department of Education.

Duke, D. (1987). *School leadership and instructional improvement.* New York: Random House.

Erickson, L. (1987). Conceptions of school culture. *Educational Administration Quarterly, 23,* 11-24.

Fieman-Nemser, S., & Floden, R. E. (1986). The cultures of teaching. In M. Wittrock (Ed.), *Handbook of research on teaching* (pp. 505-526). New York: Macmillan.

Firestone, W. A., & Louis, K. S. (1999). Schools as cultures. In J. Murphy & K. S. Louis (Eds.), *Handbook of research on educational administration* (2nd ed.). San Francisco: Jossey-Bass.

Fuhrman, S. H. (1993). The politics of coherence. In S. H. Fuhrman (Ed.), *Designing coherent education policy* (pp. 1-34). San Francisco: Jossey-Bass.

Fullan, M. (1991). *The new meaning of educational change.* New York: Teachers College Press.

Fullan, M. (1993). *Change forces.* London: Falmer.

Gersick, C. J. G., & Davis-Sacks, M. L. (1991). Summary: Task forces. In J. R. Hackman (Ed.), *Groups that work (and those that don't)* (pp. 146-153). San Francisco: Jossey-Bass.

Goodman, P. S. (1986). Impact of task and technology on group performance. In P. S. Goodman and Associates (Eds.), *Designing effective work groups* (pp. 120-167). San Francisco: Jossey-Bass.

Goodman, P. S., and Associates. (1986). *Designing effective work groups.* San Francisco: Jossey-Bass.

Hackman, J. R. (1991). Introduction: Work teams in organizations—an orienting framework. In J. R. Hackman (Ed.), *Groups that work (and those that don't)* (pp. 1-14). San Francisco: Jossey-Bass.

Hallinger, P., & Heck, R. (1996). Reassessing the principal's role in school effectiveness: A review of empirical research, 1980-1995. *Educational Administration Quarterly, 32*(1), 5-44.

Hargreaves, A., & Macmillan, R. (1991, April). *Balkanized secondary schools and the malaise of modernity.* Paper presented at the annual meeting of the American Educational Research Association, San Francisco.

Janis, I. L. (1982). *Groupthink* (2nd ed.). Boston: Houghton Mifflin.

Lareau, A. (1989). Family-school relationships: A view from the classroom. *Educational Policy, 3*(3), 245-289.

Leithwood, K. (1994). Leadership for school restructuring. *Educational Administration Quarterly, 30*(4), 498-518.

Leithwood, K. (Ed.). (2000). *Understanding schools as intelligent systems.* Greenwich, CT: JAI.

Leithwood, K., & Jantzi, D. (1990). Transformational leadership: How principals can help reform school cultures. *School Effectiveness and School Improvement, 1*(4), 249-280.

Leithwood, K., Jantzi, D., & Steinbach, R. (1995). An organizational learning perspective on schools' responses to central policy initiatives. *School Organization, 15*(3), 229-252.

Leithwood, K., Jantzi, D., & Steinbach, R. (1999). *Changing leadership for changing times.* Buckingham, UK: Open University Press.

Leithwood, K., & Joong, P. (1993). School-community relationships. In A. Hargreaves, K. Leithwood, D. Gerin-Lajoie, D. Thiessen, & B. Cousins (Eds.), *Exemplary practices in the transition years: A review of research and theory.* Report prepared for the Ontario Ministry of Education. Toronto: Ontario Institute for Studies in Education.

Leithwood, K., & Louis, K. S. (1999). *Organizational learning in schools.* Lisse, The Netherlands: Swets & Zeitlinger.

Leithwood, K., & Menzies, T. (1998a). Forms and effects of school-based management: A review. *Educational Policy, 12*(3), 325-346.

Leithwood, K., & Menzies, T. (1998b). A review of research concerning the implementation of site-based management. *School Effectiveness and School Improvement, 9*(3), 233-285.

Little, J. (1982). Norms of collegiality and experimentation: Workplace conditions of school success. *American Educational Research Journal, 19,* 325-340.

Louis, K. S., & Miles, M. B. (1992). *Improving the urban high school.* New York: Teachers College Press.

Malen, B., & Ogawa, R. T. (1988). Professional-patron influence on site-based governance councils: A confounding case study. *Educational Evaluation and Policy Analysis, 10*(4), 251-270.

McGrath, J. E. (1986). Studying groups at work: Ten critical needs for theory and practice. In P. S. Goodman and Associates (Eds.), *Designing effective work groups* (pp. 362-391). San Francisco: Jossey-Bass.

Morgan, G. (1996). Toward self-organization: Organization as brains. In *Images of organization.* Thousand Oaks, CA: Sage.

Mortimore, P., Sammons, P., Stoll, L., Lewis, D., & Ecob, R. (1988). *School matters: The junior years.* Somerset, UK: Open Books.

Murphy, J., & Beck, L. G. (1995). *School-based management as school reform: Taking stock.* Thousand Oaks, CA: Corwin.

Neck, C. P., & Manz, C. C. (1994). From groupthink to teamthink: Toward the creation of constructive thought patterns in self-managing work teams. *Human Relations, 47*(8), 929-952.

Peterson, P. L., McCarthey, S. J., & Elmore, R. (1996). Learning from school restructuring. *American Educational Research Journal, 33*(1), 119-153.

Podsakoff, P. M., MacKenzie, S. B., Moorman, R. H., & Fetter, R. (1990). Transformational leaders' behaviors and their effects on followers' trust in leader, satisfaction, and organizational citizenship behaviors. *Leadership Quarterly, 1*(2), 107-142.

Randi, J., & Corno, L. (1997). Teachers as innovators. In B. J. Biddle, T. L. Good, & I. Goodson (Eds.), *International handbook of teachers and teaching* (Vol. 2). Dordrecht, The Netherlands: Kluwer.

Roberts, N. C. (1985). Transforming leadership: A process of collective action. *Human Relations, 38*(11), 1023-1046.

Rosenholtz, S. (1989). *Teachers' workplace.* New York: Longman.

Schön, D. (1987). *Educating the reflective practitioner.* San Francisco: Jossey-Bass.

Senge, P. (1990). *The fifth discipline.* New York: Doubleday.

Shamir, B., & Howell, J. (1999). Organizational and contextual influences on the emergence and effectiveness of charismatic leadership. *Leadership Quarterly, 10*(2), 257-283.

Simon, H. A. (1996). Bounded rationality and organizational learning. In M. D. Cohen & L. G. Sproull (Eds.), *Organizational learning* (pp. 175-187). Thousand Oaks, CA: Sage.

Sitkin, S. (1992). Learning through failure: The strategy of small losses. In B. Stow & L. Cummings (Eds.), *Research in organizational behavior* (Vol. 14, pp. 231-266). London: JAI.

Snydor, J., & Ebmeier, H. (1992). Empirical linkages among principal behaviors and intermediate outcomes: Implications for principal education. *Peabody Journal of Education, 68*(1), 75-107.

Walford, G. (1993). The real lessons in school reform from Britain. *Educational Policy, 7*(2), 212-222.

Wallace, R. C., Jr. (1996). *From vision to practice: The art of educational leadership.* Thousand Oaks, CA: Corwin.

Watkins, K. E., & Marsick, V. J. (1993). *Sculpting the learning organization.* San Francisco: Jossey-Bass.

Wilson, B. L., & Corcoran, T. B. (1988). *Successful secondary schools.* East Sussex, UK: Falmer.

CHAPTER 10

Local School Districts and Instructional Improvement

Richard F. Elmore
*Graduate School of Education,
Harvard University and Consortium
for Policy Research in Education*

The Problematic Role of Local School Districts

Most public educators would find it difficult to imagine a world without local school districts, as much as they might wish that districts were better organized and run, more helpful, and less politically unstable and obtrusive. Although educators take local school districts for granted, policymakers, I think, regard them as increasingly problematical. One result of the current period of educational reform could well be a substantial erosion of the traditional role of local school districts in the governance of education, and maybe even an elimination of local school districts in all but symbolic form and function.[1]

Briefly, the problem is this: Over the past 20 years or so, states have gradually increased their share of educational funding, largely as a result of increased judicial and political pressure for equalization of local school expenditures and pressure from school districts themselves for increasingly ambitious definitions of what constitutes an "adequate" educational program. A major consequence of this gradual fiscal centralization of school finance at the state level has been increasing salience of elementary and secondary education as a state political issue and, not surprising, increasing pressure for accountability in the expenditure of state education funds. Governors and state legislators have become more active agents of

111

education reform, as much out of fiscal and political necessity as out of their own interest in the issue. The growth of the state role has been accompanied, since at least the mid-1980s, by a substantial retrenchment in federal policy, signaled by a decrease in the federal share of school funding and a shift in federal policy toward a more facilitative and less obtrusive role. Formal authority for education, then, has gradually migrated away from localities and the federal government toward states (see, e.g., Goertz, Floden, & O'Day, 1996; Massell, Fuhrman, & colleagues, 1994).

This migration of education policy and governance toward the states has been accompanied by an increasing willingness by the states to intervene directly in schools, either bypassing local school districts altogether or giving them a limited and circumscribed role. Virtually every state, for example, now has the capacity to collect school-level student performance data directly, using school districts as little more than test administration contractors, and to report school-level results at the state level. In addition, many states now directly administer rewards and penalties for school performance, with little more than symbolic participation by local administrators and school boards. Advanced reform states, such as Kentucky and South Carolina, directly administer school reward programs, independently identify schools as being in various stages of trouble on academic performance measures, and have the authority to intervene in both districts and schools to remediate poor performance (Ladd, 1996). Over time, this direct state-to-school connection will probably increase for at least two reasons: First, state policy makers are becoming less patient with educators' explanations for limited evidence of increased student performance in the face of substantially increased state expenditures. Second, local districts have been relatively defensive in the face of aggressive state reforms, responding to state initiatives for school improvement with attempts to protect their role rather than playing a more assertive role in defining the reform agenda through their own school improvement efforts.

At the same time that states have tightened the state-to-school accountability connection, they have shown themselves willing to initiate policies that directly challenge the monopoly of local school systems over the provision of public education. Many state charter school laws—in Massachusetts, for example—authorize state agencies to charter schools directly, without any local participation, or provide appeal mechanisms that permit schools to be chartered over the opposition of local districts (Finn, Bierlein, & Manno, 1996; Millot, 1996; Wohlstetter, Wenning, & Briggs, 1995). Since the late 1980s, a number of states have introduced school choice policies—postsecondary options for secondary school students, vouchers for school dropouts, interdistrict choice programs, and private school voucher programs for poor inner-city students—that allow students to move fluidly between schools of various types without regard to local jurisdictional boundaries. These programs reach only a minute fraction of students, but their effects have been disproportionately large on perceptions of the role of local school systems. State legislators have gotten used to viewing local school districts and school boards as a special interest, focused mainly on maintenance of monopoly control of public schools, and, in their view, balancing the interests of students and their parents against local institutional interests. Not surprising, local institutional interests are often the loser in these decisions.

In this political and economic climate, it is understandable that the emerging theme of state education reform is standards for student academic performance, formulated on a statewide basis, backed by rewards and sanctions that operate directly on schools, and treating school districts as agents of accountability for state-initiated policies. Standards-based reforms take as their point of departure the perceived failure of public schools to deliver reliable, high-quality instruction to all students in basic academic subjects. The distinguishing characteristic of American schools has become vast differences in the quality of teaching and learning delivered to students—within districts, from school to school; and between districts, between those with high and low proportions of students in need. These variations in student learning pose a highly conspicuous problem to state policy makers because they threaten the rationale for increased state expenditures on education.

If there is to be a reemergence of the local role in education, it will not take the form of an assertion of the traditional doctrine of local control of schools. Local districts, by becoming more fiscally dependent on states, have lost much of the power of the argument for local democratic control of schools. State legislators and governors have gotten used to making decisions that affect schools directly, and in doing so they juxtapose the institutional interests of local districts and the collective interests of professional educators against the individual interests of parents and students. State policy makers are not likely to retreat from this view, especially as pressure increases on them to account for the results of increased state expenditures. A redefinition of the local role in education will have to focus on what I have called the principle of *value added to student performance.* Like it or not, for better or for worse, the currency of the realm in education policy making has become student academic performance. States have gotten better and better at collecting school-level data on student performance and at connecting their data collection systems to state accountability systems that reward and penalize schools. They have become less and less dependent on districts to perform these functions for them. We might argue about the design of these state accountability systems, about the educational values represented in their student performance measures, or about their effects on students and schools—these arguments are legitimate and should be made. But the basic reality of education policy is, and will continue to be, that educators and the schools they work in will be judged largely by their effect on student learning. The role of local school districts will increasingly be judged—and, I think, criticized—on the basis of whether they add value to student learning.

Kenneth Leithwood has developed, in his chapter for this volume, a set of principles for continuous improvement of schools. One way of thinking about the future role of local school districts is to say that they will become the prime enablers of the school-level actions that Leithwood describes. Local school systems would organize, for example, to provide assistance to schools in clarifying their mission and goals, in reframing their cultures and structures around student learning, in collecting and using information about teaching and learning, in articulating state and district policy in ways that connect to the experience and needs of people in schools, and in creating a stable environment for planning and deliberate action. I think Leithwood's perspective on school improvement is a useful way of reframing the district role, and I would therefore recommend that district-level administrators pay attention to the school-level conditions that relate to good teaching and learning and redefine their role in terms of those actions rather than in terms of their own bureaucratic routines and institutional interests.

There is evidence that some local districts have developed effective strategies for managing school improvement on a large scale, although data on student performance suggest that these districts are a small minority. Districts that engage in effective management of school improvement tend to judge the performance of district and school administrators on the basis of their contribution to student achievement. They set clear expectations that principals will be directly involved in the curriculum and instruction in schools and will develop the competencies to make this involvement constructive; they use staff development as a deliberate instrument of instructional improvement and focus it on clearly defined district priorities; and they emphasize active involvement in instructional improvement at all levels of the district, rather than bureaucratic routine and structure (Murphy & Hallinger, 1986, 1988; Murphy, Hallinger, Peterson, & Lotto, 1987).

Yet many school districts fail to engage in constructive action around school improvement, not because they have bad intentions or even because they don't engage in activities that school people regard as constructive. School districts often fail to add value to student performance because they lack a coherent theory of how to influence teaching and learning in productive ways. This is the problem I would like to take as the focus for my contribution to this volume.

The Instructional Core and Some Ways of Improving It

The single most persistent problem of educational reform in the United States is the failure of reforms to alter the fundamental conditions of teaching and learning for students and teachers in schools in anything other than a small-scale and idiosyncratic way (Elmore 1996a). Reforms wash over schools in successive waves, creating the illusion of change on the rolling surface of policy making, but deep under this churning surface the fundamental conditions of teaching and learning remain largely unchanged in all but a small proportion of classrooms and schools (Cuban, 1984). As pressure mounts from states for increased school-level accountability for student academic performance, the problem of producing changes in teaching and learning on a large scale will become more visible and ultimately more troublesome for local school districts.

Sustained and continuous improvement in instruction on a large scale requires local educational policy makers and administrators to think and act in ways very different from in the past. Local board members and administrators have traditionally thought of themselves as responsible for the structure of relations between themselves and the schools they oversee, between teachers within schools, and between schools and their clients. Hence local policymakers and administrators have tried to influence how schools go about their work by restructuring central office functions and school-site decision making. The most common forms of restructuring have consisted of site-based management, which puts more control over decisions affecting instruction in the hands of teachers, principals, and representatives of parents and the community, and changes in the internal structure of schools that permit teachers to work more collaboratively with each other. There is substantial evidence, both historical and contemporary, that these changes in structure do not, by themselves, result in large-scale changes in teaching and learning (Elmore, 1996a; Elmore, Peterson, & McCarthey, 1996; Malen, Ogawa, & Kranz, 1990; Tyack & Cuban, 1995; Wohlstetter et al., 1995).

The reason for this gap between changes in structure and changes in teaching and learning is, in my judgment, relatively straightforward. Structural change allows teachers, principals, and community stakeholders to work together in new ways, but it does not, by itself, change the *knowledge* that these actors bring to bear on the problem of instruction. Teaching is hard work. Teachers develop their approaches to teaching out of their prior experience as students and out of their experience solving problems on a daily basis in their classrooms. These approaches to teaching tend to be relatively stable once they are established, and they are relatively immune, except in rare cases, to exhortations from policymakers and administrators to teach differently. Teachers are now being asked, by education reformers, to teach more ambitious content to larger and larger numbers of students, but these reforms do not provide teachers with access to the knowledge or support they need to practice differently. Simply changing the structure of relationships in schools does not change the knowledge of practice that teachers bring to their work. The primary problem of school reform, then, is *knowledge,* its development, use, and deployment in the classroom. Local school districts are currently not well equipped to address this problem; their long-term survival depends on their skill in addressing this problem.

Every organization has certain core processes that define its work. In schools, these core processes consist of decisions about *what* is taught; *to whom; how students are grouped* for purposes of instruction; *how content is allocated to time; how teachers relate to each other* in their work with students; and *how student learning is judged* by students, teachers, and external authorities (Elmore, 1995). Changes in schools, or in the structures that surround them, that do not affect these core processes do not affect teaching and learning. Knowledge about how to affect change in schools that does not bear on these core processes is knowledge that is not directly useful in helping teachers solve the basic problems of their daily work. Education reforms that do not give first priority to knowledge about these core processes—how they develop, how they affect what students learn, and how they affect what teachers teach—are unlikely to have any effect on student performance.

Challenging new standards for what all students should know and be able to do, in reading, writing, and mathematics, for example, can't be implemented in large numbers of classrooms without grappling with the knowledge that teachers need to change the core processes of schooling. Do new standards require new curricula? If so, where will they come from and how will teachers learn the new practices they entail? Do new standards require that students be grouped in new ways to provide them access to new curricula? If so, what sorts of grouping practices are most likely to work? Do some students require more time than others to master the academic skills represented in the standards? If so, how would time be used differently for different types of students and what would be the implications of different uses of time for the way teachers' work is organized? Do new standards require that teachers relate to each other more explicitly across grade levels, academic subjects, and groups within grade levels? If so, what kinds of coordination are required and how will they occur? Do new standards require new ways of assessing student learning and using the results of assessment to change instruction when it appears not to be working for certain kinds of students? If so, where will these new assessment practices come from? Each of these changes in the core carries with it substantial requirements for new knowledge, and their success depends on the mobilization of knowledge in forms that teachers can use in the course of their daily work.

Furthermore, changing the core processes of schooling requires an explicit theory of how teachers learn to teach and a translation of that theory into constructive actions in school systems and schools. Most school systems currently operate on the assumption that teachers arrive, early in their career, equipped to teach whatever they are expected to teach. Insofar as teachers acquire new knowledge in the course of their career, they typically do so either through single, one-shot, district-provided staff development workshops or through graduate courses in schools of education. Both of these types of training are typically delivered in isolation from the teacher's classroom and often focus on topics that have only marginal relevance to the immediate demands of classroom practice. They operate on what might call the "take-back" theory of teacher learning—that is, teachers acquire bits and pieces of knowledge from a variety of sources that they are expected to "take back" to their classrooms and implement. In the take-back theory of teacher learning, it is the teacher's sole responsibility to make sense of knowledge acquired outside the classroom and to figure out how to apply it in his or her daily work. Furthermore, it is usually the teacher's responsibility to mesh the competing demands of new knowledge delivered from a variety of sources. It is not unusual, in my experience, for a single elementary school teacher to have to figure out how to make math manipulatives, writing journals, self-esteem improvement, assertive discipline, and substance abuse education somehow cohere in a given school day.

This view of teacher learning reflects the largely confused and inept approach that most school districts take to professional development. In most local school systems, teacher professional development is organized as a separate staff function in the central office, detached from the line responsibilities by which schools are administered on a daily basis. Topics for professional development tend to reflect the current reforms du jour, and usually lack a coherent focus on a single topic over a sustained period of time. What teachers receive by way of new knowledge, then, is a welter of disconnected bits and pieces that are largely disconnected from the administrative relationships that are intended to influence their daily work.

Ann Lieberman and Lynne Miller's contribution to this volume gives an account of the current state of knowledge about the practice of professional development. My interest in the problem of professional development is in how it relates to sustained improvement of instruction. If professional development is to play a role in sustained instructional improvement, it should meet certain basic requirements. It should, for example, probably be based on the premise that teachers learn to teach—and they are likely to learn to change their teaching practice—by teaching, by engaging in new forms of practice in the presence of people who have some expertise in that practice, by observing others engaging in new forms of practice, and possibly by observing themselves on videotape and analyzing their practice with others. Professional development should probably be based on the premise that changing instruction requires coherence and focus in professional development—working, for example, on a manageable set of new practices in a sustained way over time until they become part of a relatively stable set of repertoires with which a teacher is comfortable. It should probably be based on the premise that administrators at the district and school level are responsible for creating the conditions necessary to support sustained engagement in improvement, by, for example, reducing competing demands on teachers to respond to reforms du jour, and focusing attention on a limited set of practices that are consistent with broader, systemwide expectations for student learning. And it should provide for feedback and redesign of professional development activities by teachers, based on their experience in adapting new practices to the demands of diverse classrooms. The basic theory of teacher learning here is that teachers learn to teach by teaching, but not just by improvising as solo practitioners; they learn by practicing in the presence of others and analyzing their own practice against the observed practice of others. I have seen this model work in a particularly powerful way in an urban school system (Elmore 1996b).

There may be other theories of teacher learning that are equally powerful and promising as a basis for sustained instructional improvement. I do not pretend to know the full range of possible theories that are available. My point is a broader one: It is impossible to affect teaching and learning in any sustained way across a system of schools unless the people running the system have a coherent theory of how teachers learn and are willing to base their own actions and the organization and management of the system on that theory.

This is the fundamental challenge, then, of reframing the local district's role: Basing district- and school-level decisions on an understanding of the core activities of schools and on a defensible theory of how teachers learn to teach. I offer the following two principles as guidance for administrators and teachers who are interested in pursuing this path:

1. *If it's not teaching and learning, why are we doing it?* One fundamental condition for a new district role is the understanding that everyone's job should be evaluated on the basis of its connection to the core activities of schooling and its contribution to value added to student performance. Much of the policy making and administrative activity that occurs in districts has only a remote connection to teaching and learning, and much of it complicates the jobs of teachers and principals, who bear the main responsibility for instruction, by creating a penumbra of distractions from the core problems of schooling. It is reasonable to expect that any action at the district level should be evaluated in terms of the value it adds to instruction; if it fails that standard, then it should bear a very large burden of proof.

2. *Reciprocal accountability: For performance and capacity.* As performance expectations for student learning become more explicit and more binding on schools, policymakers and administrators have a reciprocal obligation to provide the capacities necessary for school-level actors to meet these expectations. I would go so far as to say that no performance standard should be binding on teachers and principals unless system-level policymakers and administrators meet their reciprocal responsibility to provide the knowledge, professional development, and resources students need to learn what they should know and be able to do. Likewise, every professional development activity should have to meet the test of whether it connects with a specific problem of classroom practice confronting teachers in meeting expectations for student learning and whether it embodies an approach that results in the adaptation of practice to specific classroom settings.

Note

1. For criticisms of the role of local districts and proposals for reform, see Hill (1995) and Finn (1991).

References and Resources

Cuban, L. (1984). *How teachers taught: Constancy and change in American classrooms.* New York: Longman.

Elmore, R. (1993). The role of local school systems in instructional improvement. In S. Fuhrman (Ed.), *Designing coherent policy: Improving the system.* San Francisco: Jossey-Bass.

Elmore, R. (1995). Teaching, learning, and school organization: Principles of practice and the regularities of schooling. *Educational Administration Quarterly, 31,* 355-374.

Elmore, R. (1996a). Getting to scale with good educational practice. *Harvard Educational Review, 66,* 1-26.

Elmore, R. (1996b). *Staff development and instructional improvement in Community School District #2, New York City.* Cambridge, MA: Consortium for Policy Research in Education, Harvard University.

Elmore, R., Peterson, P., & McCarthey, S. (1996). *Restructuring in the classroom: Teaching, learning, and school organization.* San Francisco: Jossey-Bass.

Finn, C. (1991). *We must take charge: Our schools and our future.* New York: Free Press.

Finn, C., Bierlein, L., & Manno, B. (1996). *Charter schools in action: A first look.* Washington, DC: Hudson Institute.

Goertz, M., Floden, R., & O'Day, J. (1996). *The bumpy road to education reform* (Policy Brief No. RE-20). Philadelphia: Consortium for Policy Research in Education.

Hallinger, P., & Murphy, J. (1985). Assessing the instructional management behavior of principals. *Elementary School Journal, 86,* 217-247.

Hill, P. (1995). *Reinventing public education.* Santa Monica, CA: RAND.

Ladd, H. (Ed.). (1996). *Holding schools accountable.* Washington, DC: Brookings Institution.

Malen, B., Ogawa, R., & Kranz, J. (1990). What do we know about SBM? A case study of the literature. In W. Clune & J. Witte (Eds.), *Choice and control in American education. Vol. 2: The practice of choice, decentralization, and school restructuring* (pp. 289-342). Philadelphia: Palmer Press.

Massell, D., Fuhrman, S., with Kirst, M., Odden, A., Wohlstetter, P., Carver, R., and Yee, G. (1994). *Ten years of state education reform.* Philadelphia: Consortium for Policy Research in Education.

Millot, M. D. (1996). *Autonomy, accountability and the value of public education: A comparative assessment of charter school statutues leading to model legislation.* Seattle: Program on Reinventing Public Education, Institute for Public Policy and Management, University of Washington.

Murphy, J., & Hallinger, P. (1986). The superintendent as instructional leader: Findings from effective school districts. *Journal of Educational Administration, 24,* 213-236.

Murphy, J., & Hallinger, P. (1988). Characteristics of instructionally effective school districts. *Journal of Educational Research, 81,* 175-181.

Murphy, J., Hallinger, P., Peterson, K., & Lotto, L. (1987). The administrative control of principals in effective school districts. *Journal of Educational Administration, 25,* 161-192.

Tyack, D., & Cuban, L. (1995). *Tinkering toward Utopia: Reflections on a century of public school reform.* Cambridge, MA: Harvard University Press.

Wohlstetter, P., Wenning, R., & Briggs, K. (1995). Charter schools in the United States: The question of autonomy. *Educational Policy, 9,* 331-358.

Index

CORWIN
PRESS

The Corwin Press logo—a raven striding across an open book—represents the happy union of courage and learning. We are a professional-level publisher of books and journals for K–12 educators, and we are committed to creating and providing resources that embody these qualities. Corwin's motto is "Success for All Learners."